Extracts From The Memoranda Of Mary Hagger, Ashford, Kent

Mary Knight Hagger

EXTRACTS

FROM THE

MEMORANDA

OF

MARY HAGGER,

ASHFORD,

KENT.

"The memory of the just is blessed."—PROV. x. 7.
"Gather up the fragments that remain that nothing be lost."—JOHN v. 12.

LONDON:

HARVEY AND DARTON,
55, GRACECHURCH STREET.

1841.

THE INTRODUCTION.

WHEN the Christian example of those we love is withdrawn, and we are no longer cheered by their conversation, nor instructed by their admonitions, we recur with satisfaction to those instances of faithfulness which memory furnishes; but when assisted by written records of their devout and exercised minds, they become enhanced in value, and we esteem them as precious memorials of departed worth.

Such we believe will be the feelings of many who have known and loved the subject of this short Memoir, the reader will find for his instruction and encouragement, that in the simplicity and sincerity of her heart, she has unfolded some of her mental exercises; and as they breathe throughout the language of piety and resignation under deep and complicated trials, they will, it is hoped, afford consolation to those in similar circumstances, seeing it was by the grace of God she was what she was, and to the sustaining power of His grace, she bore testimony during a long protracted life.

In the relation of a mother few exceeded her in tenderness, and she endeavoured to attain to Christian

A 2

resignation when bereaved of her children, six of whom died at different periods.

Instructed in the school of adversity, and possessing a sympathetic mind, she was peculiarly qualified to impart consolation to the weary traveller Zionward, and to extend the hand of encouragement to those who *had* wandered from the true Shepherd—endeavouring to comfort them which were in any trouble, by the comfort wherewith she herself was comforted of God.

Deeply impressed with gratitude for the blessings with which the evening of her day was crowned, and a mind reconciled to the dispensations of Providence in earlier life, she often dwelt upon the subject in feeling remembrance of the mercies she had experienced, and to almost the latest period, her conversation and manners partook of the cheerfulness and pleasantness of her meridian life. When the awful time arrived in which she was permitted to enter her eternal rest, she passed away in sweet serenity, full of days and full of peace, and we humbly believe her redeemed spirit is numbered with those who came out of great tribulations, and have washed their robes, and made them white in the blood of the Lamb.

Ashford, 8th month, 1841.

A TESTIMONY

From FOLKSTONE MONTHLY MEETING, *concerning*
MARY HAGGER, *deceased*.

In preserving a memorial of this our dear friend, we
are instructively reminded of her meek and lowly
example; she was desirous to be found adorning the
doctrine of God her Saviour in all things; that her
rejoicing might be this, the testimony of her conscience, that with simplicity and godly sincerity, not
with fleshly wisdom, but by the grace of God, she had
her conversation in the world.

She was the daughter of our friends, William and
Lettice Knight, and was born at Stone-hall, near Wan-
stead, Essex, the 4th of 1st mo., 1758.

The following selections from her memoranda, serve
to show the early pious care of her parents. " I was
blessed with tender parents, that watched over themselves and their family with a religious care, taking
us to meetings; they were very diligent attenders
themselves, though residing at a distance of several
miles, the weather or business seldom if ever preventing." She thus adverts to her religious feelings
in early life : " I well remember being in a garden by
myself, and knew not what it was that so sweetened and
tendered by heart, that for a considerable time, I felt
as though I could not leave the spot, and several
times afterwards I took opportunities to retire, and
had similar feelings." " As I grew I often felt the
prevalence of my natural disposition, giving way too
much to indifference in things relating to my best

interest, so that I often desired something might befall
me, to arouse me from such a state of ease and unconcernedness; and after awhile, kind Providence, whose
peculiar care is extended while passing the slippery
paths of youth, inclined my heart to love Him, and
permitted me to have a fever, which in degree awakened me."

She had to pass through many painful conflicts,
often lamenting the want of an entire surrender of
heart to the refining hand of Him who was preparing
her as a vessel for his service. She was impressed
with a belief that it would be required of her to bear
public testimony to the goodness of the Lord; from
this sacrifice, she earnestly desired she might be
spared; and the language of her heart was, " Send
by whom thou wilt send, but not by me." She yielded
to this religious conviction, by giving up to speak a
few words in meetings for discipline when she apprehended it required of her. On the subject of these
meetings, she remarks, " I believe that if the discipline
is rightly supported, it must be by the influence of the
same power that moves to every duty."

Whilst having to struggle with severe outward trials,
she sought to cherish a tender conscience, and by ad-
hering to Christian principle, her conduct became
remarkable for strict integrity; and after being brought
through her temporal difficulties, by the power of
Divine Grace, she was raised up an instrument of
usefulness in the church. By abiding in deep watchfulness and humble dependence on the Lord, to know
his putting forth to the solemn work, she became qualified to speak a word in season to the weary in Zion,

and at times was strengthened to " lift up the banner on the high mountain." Her offerings in the ministry being expressed in few words, and in great diffidence and fear, were impressive, evincing that she sought not honour from others, but that which comes from the Lord alone.

In 1831, she visited by certificate the meetings in Bedfordshire and Hertfordshire, as also the families and Friends in Hertford; in the following year, she paid a similar visit to the Monthly Meetings in the county of Nottingham, and in 1835, to those composing the Quarterly Meeting of Essex: these services proved acceptable to her friends, and afforded peace to her own mind.

She felt much interested in objects of Christian philanthropy : the poor and the afflicted, more especially, obtained her commiseration. She cherished a deep solicitude for the religious welfare of her near connexions in life; desiring that they, as well as herself, might experience a growth in grace, and in the knowledge of our Lord and Saviour Jesus Christ ; thus expressing her feelings on this all-important subject, " I pray for myself and my dear children, that we may be strengthened in an unshaken belief in the efficacy of the blood of the beloved Son of God, our Lord and Saviour Jesus Christ; who came down from heaven, and took not upon Him the nature of angels, but the seed of Abraham, was born of the Virgin Mary, suffered under Pontius Pilot the cruel and shameful death of the cross, to be a propitiation and atonement for the sins of the whole world, rose again the third day from the dead, and ascended into

heaven, and is the Advocate and Mediator between
God and man, the King, High Priest, and Prophet
of his church, the author of salvation to all that obey
Him ;—true God and perfect man."

At the latter end of 1835, our dear friend was visited
with severe illness, from which her recovery then
appeared very doubtful; but she was favoured to be
restored to usual health, until the close of the following
year, when she was seized with another alarming
attack which greatly reduced her strength; yet she so
far recovered, as to be able to assemble with her friends
at religious meetings, though often under great bodily
infirmity.

During the illness above alluded to, her mind was
much clothed with love, and her expressions were often
weighty and instructive. After passing a low and
deeply depressing season, she said, "Should I be
taken now, all will be well; I have such a full·assur-
ance there is a mansion prepared for me, and that
crowns all." At another time, "It is an awful thing
to appear before the Judge of the whole earth, and I
am sure I have not a rag nor anything to cover myself with; but my whole and entire dependence is on
my holy Saviour, who I humbly hope will plead my
cause; I do believe love will cover the judgment-seat;
if there are any that slight the offers of a merciful
Saviour, how deplorable must be their condition!"
"I have felt the Comforter at the threshold of the
door, waiting to do his own office." At different
times, she expressed as follows, "I feel very low: I
want to feel more of my heavenly Father's presence.
O! I do most fervently hope, if there are any sins yet

remaining, they may be blotted out." O! how unworthy! I feel that I have not a good act of my own that I can plead; but my dear Saviour died for me; and I have a hope, that He will receive me, not of works, but of his free grace." To one of her family whom she had not seen for several days, she said, " I want to tell thee the bands are broken, and I feel great liberty in the truth, and can sometimes sing high praises." At another time, " O! that it may please my heavenly Father to say, it is enough, and take his poor, (I am almost afraid to say servant to so high a power,) to Himself."

Our beloved friend for many years suffered from a violent nervous affection of the head, accompanied with a distressing cough, which greatly exhausted her enfeebled frame, so that from the spring of 1839 to the ensuing autumn, she was almost wholly confined to the house. In the 9th mo. of that year, she received a visit from her only surviving brother, who, after a few days' illness, died at her house. After this sudden and unexpected event, her health rapidly declined, and she suffered much at times from mental depression, yet was favoured to know her heart stayed on the Lord. At one time she said, " O that I may die the death of the righteous, and that my last end may be like theirs! I have a hope that casteth out fear, I have a hope both sure and stedfast."

A few days before the final close, when alluding to the death of our blessed Saviour, she observed, " I must die the death : mine is a natural death, but His was for the whole world. He gave up his life freely,

and suffered on the cross: He gave his life a willing
sacrifice, and we must give up our whole hearts. ' No
Cross no Crown,' is a sure testimony, and will be
answered in a future day ; if we will not bear the cross,
we cannot have the crown." Then addressing her
children present, said, " O, my dear children, from
my dying bed, I beg it of you, that it may be the
constant breathing of your souls, that you may be
redeemed from the perishing things of time, and that
your affections may be fixed on eternity.—What
would it avail now, or at any other time, to have the
world, or as much as might be equal to our extravagant desires to possess ?   I would freely give it up for
a happy possession [in heaven.]   Oh press after it, do
not be satisfied in anything that is sensual or carnal,
but oh, that we may press after an inheritance in that
which will endure for ever !"   Nearly her last expressions were, " Oh eternity !—Oh the length of eternity !—Oh that it may be impressed on every heart,
the length of eternity ! there is no end."

She peacefully expired on the 25th day of the 1st
month, 1840, aged about 82 years, and is, we have no
doubt, through the blood of the everlasting covenant,
gathered to the just of all generations, to unite in
ascribing salvation to Him that sitteth on the throne,
and to the Lamb for ever more.

Her remains were interred in Friends' burial-ground
at Ashford, on the 2nd day of 2nd month, 1840.

Given forth by Folkstone Monthly Meeting, held at
Canterbury, the 12th of the 3rd month, 1840.

EXTRACTS, &c.

I was blessed with tender parents [William and Lettice Knight] who watched over themselves and their families with religious care, endeavouring to keep us out of unsuitable company and to protect us from harm, taking us frequently to meetings; and were themselves very constant attenders, though residing at a distance of several miles, the weather or business seldom, if ever, preventing. My dear mother filled the station of elder: she was an upright hearted woman, remarkable for her integrity. My father was a minister, a man of an humble and contrite spirit, that feared God and hated covetousness; he was a good example to those about him, and much beloved by his friends.

In my early age, I was sensible of the tendering impressions of divine love. I well remember being in the garden by myself, and knew not what it was that so sweetened and affected my heart, that for a considerable time, I felt as though I could not leave the spot; and several times afterwards I took opportunities to retire, and had similar feelings.

As I grew older, I often felt the prevalence of an easy natural disposition, too much, far too much, giving way to indifference in things relating to my best interest, so that I often desired something might befall me to arouse me from such a spirit of ease and unconcernedness ; and after a while kind Providence, whose peculiar care is extended over us, whilst passing the slippery path of youth, inclined my heart to love Him, and permitted me to have an illness which continued some weeks, and in degree awakened me.

About the fifteenth year of my age, I was sent to school, to Martha Winter, (afterwards Routh) of Nottingham, whom I much esteemed. She was concerned to example her family in the path of humility, and carefully watched over herself, lest any thing like passion should arise when cross occurrences happened. This striving against natural disposition and temper was a striking example in her, truly worthy of imitation, and caused those under her care to serve her from love rather than fear.

While (at school) I was beset with temptations to evil, the envier of my comfort, often drew my mind into carelessness and forgetfulness of that precious influence I had been favoured with, which would have gathered and kept me within the fold, had it been attended to. Tenderness of heart was, in mercy, sometimes granted; and I often repented in the night of the commissions of the day. Many hours I have been awake, pressed with painful feelings, whilst my companion has been asleep. Dear Martha, who always manifested a Christian care over us, was one evening, after reading, particularly led to supplicate for the preservation of the children of believing parents, in which these words were uttered, " Oh!

prepare them to appear before thee, clothed in white, that their parents may have to say, ' Here are we with those that thou hast given us' "—which words sunk deep into my heart, knowing that I had religious parents. I often got alone, and begged for preservation. One day, hearing a boy in the street using grievous expressions and making use of the Sacred Name, I trembled, and breathed to my gracious Protector to preserve me from such hardness of heart.

The prospect of leaving school, which occurred about two years after, was a trial to me, believing that I should be exposed in various ways, some time after which I went to reside with my uncle, John Stanley, at a farm of my father's about three miles distance: he was a solid conscientious man, much given to retirement, often walking alone in solitary places, and justly merited the testimony borne of him at his funeral, "An Israelite indeed in whom there is no guile." He died the 22nd of 2nd mo. 1782. During my residence with him, I was much tossed with tempest and not comforted, and tried with temptations which were permitted almost to overwhelm me; yet being much alone my heart was often poured out in secret to a compassionate Saviour for preservation, and I was at times favoured to partake, in some degree, of those joys with which a stranger cannot intermeddle. My parents frequently came and spent a while with us. One day my father was sitting looking into the garden, and called me to him to shew me the bough of an apple tree which was bent down by the weight of fruit that was upon it, very instructively remarking, that fruit bearing branches must bow to the root of life in themselves.

About this time, it pleased unerring wisdom to take to himself my dear uncle, who had a tender care over me, we often walked about four miles to meeting together, and he would sometimes enter into serious conversation by the way; and I believe would have loved me sincerely if I (like himself) had submitted to a self-denying life; but my spirit wanted much bringing down and humbling. In the day I was much employed; in the night I often felt sad, and watered my pillow with my tears: belief also fixed on my mind that it would be required of me to tell to others that "the Lord is good," for indeed I felt him so. I had many comforts as well as hidden exercises, which none knew but the Lord alone. The cry of my heart was, " Send by whom thou wilt send, send not by me."

In the year 1782, I married Stephen Hagger of Hertford, I saw difficulty and trouble in my way, and so did my affectionate father for me, yet he with myself believed, if I kept near the Fountain of Life I should be preserved, and I can truly say, that my heart was much humbled by the consideration that I did what I *believed* was my *duty;* and as I was about to leave my father's house outwardly, strong cries were raised, that my heavenly Father might be near, which in adorable mercy I experienced in proportion to my attention to the " still small voice."

It pleased providence to take my dear father, on the 30th of 11th mo. 1787, from a state of much bodily suffering to that of never-ending joy. I spent about six weeks with him during his last illness, which has afforded me many comfortable reflections. He had his servants called in as he found his strength would bear, and gave them advice suitable to their station, pressing upon them to persevere in a steady care, to act honestly, &c. For us, his children, he also felt an earnest solicitude, that we might be careful to live in the fear of the Lord, and be a help and comfort one to another and to our aged mother. He was favoured with a calm and peaceful mind, and had full assurance of eternal happiness, which he expressed in much tenderness to several Friends who came to see him. At one time, he said, he could adopt the language of the apostle, "I have fought a good fight, I have finished my course, I have kept the faith; henceforth there is laid up for me a crown of righteousness, which the Lord, the righteous Judge, shall give me at that day, and not to me only, but unto all them also that love his appearing."

I felt the loss of my father much; few loved a parent better, and few were blessed with one more worthy. Soon after this, my dear mother began to decline, and died in about two years. She enjoyed a resigned mind, and there was every reason to believe she made a happy close.

I was now bereaved of both my parents, my family increased, and my trials also: I felt that I had none

to look to but the Lord alone, no helper like him in
times of trouble. The weighty prospect before mentioned overwhelmed all other concerns, although I
had given up to speak a few words in meetings of
discipline when Truth required it of me. I believe if
the discipline is rightly supported, it must be by the
influence of the same Power that moves to every
duty; and I have been sorry to observe in some, a disposition to be active therein, without waiting long
enough at Wisdom's gate: these have misled the
weak, and hurt the pure cause. In this time of deep
exercise, I cried to my gracious Redeemer that the
weight might be taken from me, and laid on some one
more worthy: I knew myself entirely unfit, and
I longed to find an easier way to the kingdom than
by the cross, and by appearing and feeling so much a
fool before men. Oh! it is indeed a strait gate and a
narrow path, to that part in us that is unmortified, and
will not bear the cross; but the resigned mind finds a
precious liberty in the truth, and that there is no joy
like the joy of God's salvation. One time when
taking a solitary walk, a contriting impression covered
me with a sense of duty: after some time of resistance,
hearing the intelligible voice, "Wilt thou neither be
faithful in sight nor out of sight?" I kneeled down
in the path, and though I uttered no words, the
weight I felt was such, that I believe I should not
have risen had any one passed me. For many days
after this, my mind enjoyed sweet peace.

Thus I went on a long time, passing through many
hidden baptisms. My dear friend, Mary Prior, of

Hertford, was a tender mother to me, she resided near, and was my constant attendant in many difficulties. One time when my father was present, she addressed him very encouragingly, and supplicated that a double portion of his spirit might rest upon his daughter. But oh! my remissness and falling off from duty many ways! I was one of a sad heart, and very apt to be cast down, and the envier of my peace did not fail to use all his limited power to keep me so, and presented many discouragements to my view, such as that I had many times been unfaithful, and they who were rightly called were willing. This I knew to be a truth, but I did not consider that I was made willing by the power of the cross. Oh! he is a liar, and ever was! Mayst thou, my gracious Helper, never suffer my poor tossed soul to become a prey to his cruel malice! It was about seven years from the first time that the belief had been sealed on my mind, that it would be required of me to expose myself in public, when one morning before I rose from my pillow, the impression fixed with me that next First day morning would be the time to make a total surrender; and till then, the burden was so heavy upon me, I could hardly set one foot before another in my family, and I craved for strength to stand in my proper allotment. After the meeting had been gathered awhile, the words presented, Lord, take away my stony heart, and give me a heart of flesh, a heart sincerely devoted to serve thee. The impression was accompanied by a belief that if I did not give up, the temptations that I had been so long at times tried with would be permitted to come upon me with double force. I gave up, and after the meeting my mind was favoured with a covering of quietness and love that I cannot express. That day two weeks my soul was humbled in prayer, I felt as if something drew me on my knees : these acts of dedication, small compared to many, caused peace and love to flow in my heart to my family and friends. I thought within myself, if I could but continue in this state, and partake of the bitter cup, the wormwood and the gall, no more, I should then have something like a heaven upon earth : but this is not the place of our rest.

[It appears that she was acknowledged a minister by Hertford Monthly Meeting, in the 4th mo., 1794. In the year 1797, she removed with her husband and family to Enfield highway, within the compass of Tottenham Monthly Meeting. About this time, she felt drawings in her mind to pay a religious visit to Friends in Essex, but through lending an ear to the suggestions of her soul's enemy, she did not resign herself to this apprehension of duty, and thus incurred the displeasure of her heavenly Father, causing herself afterwards (as she has been heard to say with tears) a long wilderness travel of many years, in which troubles and trials outwardly, as well as desertion and distress inwardly, were her sorrowful portion. Their outward circumstances were greatly reduced, and though she exerted herself to the utmost in assisting to support her family, all her attempts appeared unsuccessful, and there were times when they *were greatly* distressed. The enemy of her soul did not fail to make

use of these trials, to plunge her discouraged mind
still lower, and she resigned her seat in the meeting
of ministers and elders in the year 1807. In the year
1809, she lost a very promising child; and in 1810, she
attended the death bed of her husband, who after much
conflict of mind, was favoured to make a peaceful
close. But He who waits long to be gracious, and
will have mercy on his afflicted children, was pleased
in due time to say, it is enough, and to favour her
again, both with the lifting up of the light of His
blessed countenance, and with a gradual increase of
outward substance; whereby she was enabled to discharge all her debts, and many of her husband's also.
Yet, although thus favoured, and again permitted to
feel the influence of the Divine Spirit, constraining
her to testify of the Lord's goodness to others, many
still were her discouragements, and frequent work was
made for fresh repentance, in the fearful withholding
of more than was meet, the retracing of her steps
requiring more faith than a simple acting at first had
done; and she thus expresses herself in after life, in
reverting to this long time of trial—" I have abundant
cause to admire and reverence the Great Name, that
His preserving arm has been round about me, and His
tender mercies are lengthened out still. When I have
been mourning over my own infirmities, I have fully
believed, had I been more resigned, the grand enemy
could not have caused so long a wilderness; but he
knows I am one of a sad heart, and very apt to take
discouragement, and never more so than of late : were
it not for the sweet feeling of peace mercifully granted,
when ability is afforded to give up to requirings of

duty (as I apprehend) my little faith, like poor Peter's, would fail, and I should sink under the weight of my frequent unwatchfulness, and want of more firm resolution."

In reviving these circumstances, which she would often speak of to her intimate friends, with tears of gratitude to Him who had delivered her out of all her afflictions, it is hoped that warning, instruction, and encouragement may be derived by the reader; at the same time we feel it like rearing a little altar of praise to Him whose compassions fail not, but who enables the upright to hold on their way, fixing their hearts in humble trust on Him alone.]

My brother, William Knight died the 17th of 2nd mo., 1814, in his 58th year. "Mark the perfect man, and behold the upright; for the end of that man is peace." He was buried at Chelmsford; a very large and quiet meeting was held on the occasion, which was graciously owned by the presence of Him who visited this my dear brother, and inclined his heart to seek and serve Him during a life of affliction, and through whose mercy he has no doubt entered the kingdom of everlasting rest.

8th mo. 4th. Dear A. S. was buried at Tottenham: S. G. was at the interment, it was a memorable time, he was much favoured in testimony, and the meeting also with a sweet calm.

2nd mo. 26th, 1815. Returned from the funeral of Mary Pryor. She might justly be termed "a mother in Israel," evidently feeling true love to clothe her heart, and in it endeavouring to cherish the least appearance of good in all. Her general life and conversation was edifying and reaching; her reverent awful waiting in silent meetings was often an excitement to diligence; her ministry, deep and powerful, has often roused a longing of soul in some who were favoured to be intimately acquainted with her, for ability to follow her as she followed Christ the Captain of the saints' victory.

10th. Poor and low, but not forsaken. When a little feasting has been permitted, Oh! my soul, be thou willing to fill up thy part of suffering, for His sake who died to purchase everlasting life for thee.

After about a month's confinement by inflammation of my eyes, they are now restored. Oh! that this afflicting circumstance may awaken my gloomy mind to more diligence, that the awful sound may never be heard in mine ears, "The summer is ended, the harvest is past, and thou art not saved!"

28th. My sister and myself left home to visit our relations in Essex, and were at Chelmsford meeting on fourth day. I felt very poor and forsaken, lamenting my backwardness to duty, and longed for more strength and faith. May I endeavour more and more for ability to adopt the language, " Let others do as they may, as for me and my house, we will serve the Lord." We were out about three weeks, and I returned home better satisfied than I had reason to expect, having renewed cause to admire the tender dealings of a faithful Creator.

6th mo. 25th. Attended the funeral of F. P. She had been at meeting in usual health, went to bed, and died in her sleep : an awful but [doubtless] a happy change for her. May so striking an event arouse us careless ones to more watchfulness, and prove an excitement to make our calling and election sure.

7th mo. 9th. Monthly Meeting—I believed it right for me to bear testimony to the exemplary life of our late dear friend F. P., and was rewarded with peace.

8th mo., 26th. My dear daughter Elizabeth was taken ill: little did I think that her illness would prove fatal. After about eleven days' deep suffering, she was, without the shadow of a doubt, happily released on the 4th of 9th mo. Oh! the anguish and distress I felt, is beyond words to express: her mind was preserved quiet and calm, and her end was blessed. The funeral took place at Tottenham, on the 9th, a meeting was held on the occasion. " Blessed are the dead that die in the Lord." Shall we call in question the ways of the Almighty, or hesitate to believe that the Judge of all the earth doeth right? I had previous to this affliction, been advised to try sea air to recover my health, my son and daughter who resided at Ashford, persuaded me to return with them, from whence I went on to Folkstone, where I stayed about a month, and spent it in the bitterness of my soul. Oh! may the everlasting arm continue to be underneath in all our afflictions, give us strength to trust in Him, to fear Him, and to take courage.

[Extract from a letter written to a friend at this time.]

MY DEAR FRIEND,

I hope it will be excusable, if in the bitterness of my heart I unfold a little into thy bosom, whom I have long looked to as a father in experience, and have ere now had much consolation in thy communications; though in the present conflict, I feel afraid to look or wish for it from any quarter, but the true source of everlasting help; and that seems withheld or dried up,—it is as a fountain sealed. Oh! had I strength to believe His mercies are continued, His loving-kindness lengthened out still, then I should have hope. But now I seem overwhelmed, the depression of my mind is heavier than I know how to bear, and temptation follows me; the envier of my peace is indeed as a roaring lion seeking to devour the good, if any ever prevailed. Oh! that I could feel my confidence again renewed in that everlasting Helper, whom I have of late believed it my duty to recommend to others, more frequently than has been the case some years past, but have felt greater discouragement of late than words can express, sometimes giving up pretty freely, sometimes holding back a part.

If I had it in my power I dare not call my dear Elizabeth back again: I know it is a duty to stand resigned to every dispensation of Divine Providence, but I cannot attain it. I wish I could hide myself in a cave of the earth, where I could mourn out my days in sorrow, and see man no more; or that the Almighty would be pleased to support with his life-giving presence, while the waves and the billows pass over. I often desire to have my punishment in this life, if I may but enjoy the enriching presence of Him whom my soul hath loved when these few moments of affliction, of pain and sorrow are over.

Oh! that we, dear ———, may have our rest secured where the wicked cease from troubling, and where the weary find rest. I have been afraid to desire help, except from Him who alone knows I feel unable to offer a sigh or a tear, or scarcely to breathe for help; but may He who cares for the sparrows, in His own time, care for me, and others who are tried as to an hair's breadth.

Thy affectionate friend,

M. HAGGER.

10th mo. 29th. Quarterly Meeting, it was large and satisfactory, many little seasonable offerings in the fore part, towards the end, dear B. W. sweetly addressed a hidden, afflicted state, and several times expressed encouragement to such, to hold on their way. After which S. H. concluded the meeting in supplication, which I consider the most solemn worship attainable.

After a considerable time of hesitation about going to Ashford, I left home for that purpose 28th of 1st. mo. 1818.—My mind on the way was so calm and peaceful as caused me to think I was not out of my place.

6th mo. 1820. At the last Yearly Meeting, many sensibly felt the extendings of Divine regard. S. G. who is lately returned from Russia, and J. A. visited the women's meeting, and had a very instructive testimony, recommending us to a state of passiveness, as clay in the hands of the potter, and to become passive even as the mire in the streets.

S. G. left London soon after, and returned to the bosom of his friends.

10th mo. 21st. How unspeakably awful is the prospect of a never-ending existence, one that cannot change! and how are the branches of our family cut down as on the right hand and on the left!

I spent a few days pleasantly with my kind friend E. H. at Hertford: we went to see a friend in declining health, sat a little time together, and were refreshed. We dined with a relation. A few words solemnly impressed me, and though to give up, felt as near as that of parting with a right hand or a right eye, it was sealed on my mind, that if I did not bear the cross, I should not obtain the crown. On my return, I seemed as though I had been sitting under my own vine and under my own fig-tree, where none shall make afraid. After meeting, I returned home. In a little retirement this morning, I was owned with the precious feeling of good which I covet above all things. O Lord, preserve me in the decline of life from a state of gloom and insensibility, and grant a lively hope in thy mercy.

1st mo. 23rd, 1825. ———'s child was buried at Tottenham. After meeting, my poor unwatchful mind fell into deep distress, through neglect of attending to the still small voice, or inclination to be with them at the grave side. Oh! the heart-felt pain that followed me. " If thy own heart condemn thee, God is greater." I begged for mercy and strength to rise above the fear of my fellow-creatures.

24th. I was favoured with a little more calm,

B

and opened the Bible on the 42nd Psalm, 11th verse, "Why art thou cast down, O my soul? and why art thou disquieted within me? hope thou in God, for I shall yet praise him who is the health of my countenance and my God." Towards morning my stubborn will gave way a little, and I had a sweet sleep. It is a mercy to know our sins to go before hand to judgment, and to feel the poor tossed mind stayed on a faithful Creator.

2nd mo. 5th, 1825. Standing by the grave of J. M., I felt a necessity to expose myself. I returned home with the reward of peace, which humbled my mind under a sense of forgiveness for my former withholding.

10th mo. 11th. Returned from Kent, where I spent about nine weeks pleasantly, and I hope not grown worse in best things.

11th mo. 2nd. I have had for about a week past a violent attack of nervous head-ache; my outward prospects on account of health are dull and gloomy. Oh! may my soul be more firmly established on that Rock that is both sure and stedfast.

13th. After feeling a pressing necessity I kneeled down by poor afflicted J. M.'s bedside, and I hope rightly petitioned for him and myself, that we might not be forsaken in old age and affliction. The reflection of this opportunity afforded me much satisfaction.

1826, 9th mo. 18th. Returned from Ashford where I had spent six weeks much to my satisfaction, and three weeks at Folkstone—part of the time in illness, which though painful was not unprofitable,—wherein

I had to admire the tender dealings of the Most High;
I have no reason to regret my visit to this place, I was
by myself, which is what I have long wished to be,
and I was favoured with some sweet refreshing seasons
in my secret retirements.

1st mo. 26th, 1827. O thou who hast in abundant mercy condescended to be the guide of my
early age, when under the care of tender parents,
I have abundant cause to commemorate thy loving-
kindness and Fatherly care over me: if I had been
in all things faithful to thy commands, how would
my peace have flowed as a river, although I have
painfully to reflect on many omissions and commissions, I have many times experienced that there
is mercy with Thee that Thou mayst be feared.
And now I pray thee to be the support of my old
age. Oh! cause my mind to be fixed on Thee,
Thou everlasting rock of ages.

4th mo. 4th. Thou who hast all power in thy
hand, in heaven and on earth, oh! that it would please
thee so to humble my heart, that I might have no
will of my own, but feel perfect resignation to thy
holy will in all things, Thou hast promised a blessing
to the poor in spirit, forget not one who is as a worm
and no man before thee. The distressing pain in my
head is very trying to bear, grant patience, and cause
it to prove as a refiner's fire and as a fuller's soap.

7th mo. 16th. This morning the pain in my head
was very distressing, I was low, thinking the awful
summons was at hand. I was however favoured to feel
calm and quiet, and endeavoured to pray for perfect

resignation, and " that I might die the death of the righteous, and that my last end might be like his."

Perusing the writings of our worthy predecessors often proves instructive. My heart was affected this day in reading some of the life of John Crook, where I found this striking passage, which he copied from the margin of an old Bible, printed about the year 1599, " When the mind thinks nothing, when the soul covets nothing, and the body acteth nothing contrary to the will of God, this is perfect sanctification."

TO A FRIEND.

Ashford,   1827.

MY DEAR FRIEND,

Thy affectionate lines were truly acceptable, it is indeed a consolation to believe we are not alone in the tribulated path. Job Scott calls it "an old beaten path." I well remember your kindness to me long since, and when thou feelst an inclination to drop a mite (as thou callst it) do not withhold ; remember the effect of a small instrument formerly, when the command was given to sound the rams' horns, and the people joined in the shout. I believe little offerings are as humiliating to give up to as longer testimonies, and if it is all that is required, the reward is sure.

[Speaking of her apprehension of duty to appear in meetings, she says,] The awful engagement has been a gradual exercise to me from early life, none knew the pantings of my heart; I could not let Him go, and my stubborn, disobedient will would not give up to serve Him freely; if my life had been required, it would have been an easier sacrifice. I have for many months and years gone bowed under these humiliating feelings, begging that the impression might be taken from me, and laid on some one more fit. I have abundant cause to admire and reverence the Great Name, that His preserving arm has been round about, and His tender mercies are lengthened out still. I much desire, my dear friend, to be preserved from a wish to live on the labour of others, but to be resigned to do the work assigned me, and to be strengthened, now in my declining age, and made sensible of forgiveness for many omissions that are passed, (oh! what a happy state!) and in future to make strait steps to the land of rest. I should like thee to mention the subject of my leaving Tottenham to ——; I have a great opinion of her judgment, and love her much; she will, I hope, as well as thyself, weigh the matter for me; it seems no light thing; and if she or thyself have a few words for me, it will be acceptable: if it is reproof, I can bear it, and if encouragement, I hope it will do me good. When thou art favoured with ability for prayer, or panting for preservation, remember thy poor unworthy friend,

MARY HAGGER.

[This year, 1827, she removed to Ashford, within the compass of Folkstone Monthly Meeting, and was re-acknowledged a member of the Select Meeting in 5th mo. 1830.]

3rd mo. 19th. I arrived safe at Newington, and found

my dear children well. Not having been at Tottenham
for a considerable time, I felt a renewed regard for
many friends whom I had known and loved, many
years before I left, I called and took leave of several,
in two families a few words arose as a sacrifice called
for, and obedience procured the reward.

Looking towards our little meeting at Ashford, my
mind is affected with weighty reflections, how shall so
poor a creature as I go in and out, so as to give no
occasion of stumbling to the honest inquirer. Truly
the fields appear white unto harvest in many places,
may the Great Husbandman be pleased, in the riches
of his love to raise up, *qualify*, and *send many faithful
labourers* into his harvest. Oh! for a deeper sense of
gratitude than I have yet known. Great and mar-
vellous are thy works, O Lord, past finding out by
thy poor creatures!

After my return home, I fell into much poverty of
spirit, I seemed to have no strength to feel after what
I had so often coveted, and striving to wait in the
quiet, these words presented, " I am a stranger in the
earth, hide not thy commandments from me." " Will
the Lord cast off for ever? will he be favourable no
more? Is his mercy clean gone for ever? Doth His
promise fail for ever more? Hath God forgotten to
be gracious? Hath He in anger shut up his tender
mercies?" These words of the Psalmist raised in me
similar pantings of heart. Mayst Thou, O Lord!
be my shield, and the lifter up of my head.

8th mo. 1st. We were favoured with a visit from
J. H——, of Lancashire, who is visiting the county.

Our little company met on sixth day evening, and we were favoured with a heart-tendering season. His appearance and exemplary conduct afforded a striking example of humility and self-denial. The company of dedicated servants thus sent, I consider, as a renewed visitation of Divine Love.

After this visit, distress and woe again became my bitter cup. I looked back on many circumstances of my chequered life with doubting and fear. Thick darkness covered me. I sought Him whom, in the days of my youth, I loved above all other enjoyments; but He had hid his face from me. I sought Him by night and by day, but found him not. The God and Father of the faithful (in which number I know I cannot include my disconsolate soul) is not dealing with me according to my deserts, but according to his own loving-kindness and tender mercy. " I will (saith the Lord) bring the blind by a way that they know not, and lead them in paths that they have not known : I will make darkness light before them, and crooked paths straight; these things will I do unto them, and will not forsake them." " I will go before thee and break in pieces the gates of brass, and cut the bars of iron asunder, and will give thee the treasures of darkness, and the hidden riches of secret places." How precious are the Scriptures when opened by their Divine Original! they are as honey from the rock, yea, sweeter than the honey-comb.

18th. I have been tried much, for about the last two weeks, by indisposition, which brought me very low; my bodily strength failed, and my little stock of

faith was tried to an hair's breadth. The volume of
the book within and without seemed sealed as with
seven seals, that none could open but the Lion of the
tribe of Judah, who can quicken the dead, and call
the things which are not as though they were. Oh!
that I could come into His presence, and plead with
Him, as a man pleadeth with his friend; for though
I see Him not, yet judgment is with Him; therefore,
O my soul, trust thou in Him.

8th mo. 22nd. I was sitting by myself (in my son's
cottage, near Ashford), whether I was dozing or not,
I cannot tell. I had sat but a short time, when I saw
my dear father as plainly as ever I did when living,
dressed in light clothes, such as he used to wear, and
a neck-cloth about his neck, without his hat; he
appeared to be about three or four yards from me; the
clear shining light of the place where he was, also the
beautiful serenity and composure of his countenance
exceeded anything I ever saw, nor can I describe it
to another. He looked at me, and very sweetly smiled.
The vision was of short duration, but it brought an
awe that affected my heart with tenderness and solemnity. Oh! that myself and my beloved children may
be permitted to go down again and again to the very
bottom of Jordan, the river of God's judgment, that
we may be cleansed from every defilement, and the
precious part in us be prepared to unite with those, who
are already centred in happiness, in a song of praise.

9th mo. 7th. Attended a preparative meeting, the
fore part of which was deeply exercising; but before
we separated, light broke forth and dispersed the

cloud, and enabled us in effect to adopt the language of the woman formerly, " Rejoice with me for I have found the piece that was lost."

23rd. Our Quarterly Meeting was held about this time at Maidstone. A solemn quiet prevailed, and I believe the meeting was preciously owned, particularly in the fore part. I came home in the evening poorly in health, and stripped and low in mind, though I felt no condemnation. Surely the tendering love of Him who dwelt in the bush is present every where if sought after. It is so prevalent in our little meetings, where six or seven assemble, that I sometimes long for a meeting day. Oh! may we, in deep humility, number our blessings, and prize our inestimable privilege of sitting together without interruption, from any form of words.

29th. My health in the course of this week has been improved; but where has been the return of gratitude to the preserver of men, who bringeth down to the grave and lifteth up? Like the unstable element whose billows run very high, and wave succeeds to wave, so rest and quiet seem to take their leave of us; but man did not make himself, neither can he deliver or preserve himself; yet I believe in those seasons of deep distress poor mortals are under the immediate and particular care of the Most High; and, in the language of one of his favoured servants, we may say, " There are none so near fainting but he putteth his arm under their head." " He marketh our wanderings and knoweth the path we take."

1st mo. 4th, 1828. Still poorly, hardly able to sit

c 3

meeting, or do my share of labour therein. Oh!
that a faithful Creator would see fit to release me
from this poor diseased tabernacle, that through the
merits of a dear Redeemer the precious part might
ascend to him who gave it! How hast Thou broken
in and tendered my heart!

10th mo. 21st. I can say thy rod and thy staff
they comfort me. Surely Jehovah is good to Israel,
graciously regarding the low state of those that seek
him, and that think upon his name. He knoweth
our frame and remembereth that we are dust. Oh!
through all and every trying exercise, may the
seed sown in much debility grow till mortality be
swallowed up of life!

5th mo. 18th. I left home for Maidstone, and
next day reached Tottenham, intending to be at the
Yearly Meeting; but was so unwell that most of the
time was spent there. Thou, who doest all things
well, canst bring near to the grave, and raise up at
thy pleasure. Under every permission of thy providence, strengthen my heart with increasing faith to
trust and not be afraid. I have nothing that I can
return unto thee for thy abundant and adorable
mercies, nor have I any hope of admission into thy
kingdom of rest and peace, but through the intercession of thy dear and beloved Son, who taketh away
the sins of the world, who was wounded for our transgressions, who was bruised for our iniquities, and by
whose stripes we are healed. I was, however,
favoured to attend three of the sittings of the Yearly
Meeting, staid from home till the 10th of 7th mo.,

and was so far recovered as to be able to return to Ashford.

7th mo. 15th. Lying on the bed, very low and poorly, I was favoured to look towards the God of patience and consolation; my heart was tenderly affected with love for the whole creation, for whom our dear Redeemer suffered, and for my own affectionate children with their near connexions in particular. Oh! may they be blessed with the dew of heaven, may the blessing of the everlasting hills rest upon them! My mind returned to its own exercise, in which a sweet calm was felt, and I rejoiced, with many tears, in the God of my salvation.

9th mo. 2nd. In sitting in our little meeting to-day, I thought I never felt my mind more replenished with love to our holy Helper, from whom are all our well-springs; and also to the few with whom I was gathered. Coming home and speaking to a friend, I got off my guard, which caused leanness and poverty, though not much distress; which will be the case till every obstruction be removed, and infinite goodness is pleased to take full possession of the heart, and to bind the strong man, spoiling all his goods.

Two very dull meetings: some desire was felt to wait on the holy Helper, in absolute dependence, in nothingness of self; but something seemed like a bar in the way: much rubbish is collected, that prevents our getting into the closet and shutting to the door.

10th mo. 18th. I felt pain of heart for want of more attention to the still small voice, in our afternoon meeting. O Thou who art the Helper of the poor and the needy in their distress, be pleased to cause my heart to be more and more subject to Thy blessed will, that so I may be permitted to partake of Thy internal presence, which is better than life. " Who is a God like unto Thee, who pardoneth iniquity, and passeth by the transgression of the remnant of thine heritage? Thou retaineth not thine anger for ever, because thou delighteth in mercy.

10th mo. 21st. At our little meeting I felt more calm and serene than sometimes. He that allureth into the wilderness can open a door of hope, for ever blessed be his name! Oh! that I possessed more of the spirit of Caleb and Joshua, who followed the Lord fully, and through faith and patience inherited the promised land.

12th mo. 14th. I attended a Quarterly Meeting at Folkstone, and believe many were sensible of feelings resembling the mantle cast over Elisha formerly. What a privilege we enjoy! May none professing with us forsake [Christ] the fountain of living water, who said " If any man thirst let him come unto me and drink," and turn aside to the corrupt channels of carnal reason and creaturely power; for if so, the strong shall be as tow, and the maker of it as a spark, when the Lord shall shake terribly the earth, and exalt his only begotten Son as the refuge of the poor, and the strong-hold of the daughter of Sion.

23rd. I met at our week day meeting with three besides myself, and much desired that the drawing back of others might not operate to discourage any.

The blessing is not confined to the multitude, and if
we are so favoured as to meet with the beloved of souls,
the chief of ten thousand, we may rejoice that we
have found the pearl of great price.

1st mo. 8th, 1829. I heard of the death of J. B.
When I consider how many way-marks on our walls
are removed, and view with awfulness the shade of
dissolution as at the threshold of my door, oh! that.
I could possess an unshaken hope that a standard will
be raised up against the king of terrors, so that death
may be a welcome messenger, as was the case with
our dear ancient Friend, who is gathered into the
garner of everlasting rest, as a shock of corn in its
season!

2nd mo. 6th. Commences the seventy-second
year of my age. Through unutterable mercy I have
numbered many days, compared with the generality
of the human race, and yet, on looking back, I am
ready to say, few and evil have been the days of
the years of my pilgrimage; I find I have neither
storehouse, nor barn, nor a rag to cover my many
errors, but all are open and bare to the view of
Him with whom we have to do, and who comforted
his followers by reminding them, that they were of
more value than many sparrows.

3rd mo. 21st. I went to Dover to the funeral of
———— who left a sweet babe about nine days old.
A watchful providence owned some of our minds
with a fresh feeling of his goodness, which is ancient
and new, whereby a consoling hope was entertained
of the eternal well-being of the deceased, that her

tears strewed in secret were accepted, and that she
now has the blessed enjoyments of that city, where
none can say I am sick. But unto such as still go
mourning on their way, saying, " Spare thy people,
O Lord, and give not thy heritage to reproach,"
He is giving at times, to experience the oil of joy
for mourning, and the garment of praise for the
spirit of heaviness ; these are of that number " who
did all eat of the same spiritual meat, and did all
drink of the same spiritual drink, for they drank of
that spiritual Rock that followed them, and that
Rock was Christ."

5th mo. 12th, 1830. Our Monthly Meeting was
held at Ashford, a memorable day to me.* May
the God of all grace, in his unmerited condescension,
so watch over and stay my mind, that I may give no
offence, either to Jew or Gentile, or bring dishonour
on his church or people !

17th, second day. On the first sitting down of
the Yearly Meeting, we were favoured with a precious
covering, my mind was humbled under a sense of
its many deficiencies, of how much I owe, and that I
possess nothing that I can offer in return for such
unspeakable blessings.

The meeting ended on the seventh day week by a
meeting of ministers and elders in the morning.
Reflecting on such dignified stations has often affected
my heart. " Watch and pray," has sweetly occurred
to my mind, and for this good end, " that ye enter

* The day in which she was reinstated a Minister by Folkstone
Monthly Meeting.

not into temptation;" by which the vessel may be preserved in sanctification and honour, and the immortal birth have its habitation in a purified temple. Then may the new heavens and the new earth break forth into singing, because the Lord comforteth his people, and hath mercy on his afflicted. We returned home and attended the Quarterly Meeting at Dover, it was a time of feeding in a good degree, so that many could say, in the disciples' language, that they lacked nothing.

Thou hast, O gracious Father! condescended in the days of my youth to visit my soul, and incline it to seek thy tendering presence, [whereby] I have often felt as a worm, and no man before thee—thou hast been (according to my attention to thy inspeaking word) a sure guide, a director, and deliverer in various trials and difficulties; and now in my declining age, when health and strength fail, I crave thy merciful assistance and protection, that so thy light, that was a light to David's feet and lantern to his path, may be mine, and prove the joyful theme of my evening song.

7th mo. 14th. My son and daughter being gone to the Monthly Meeting, I went to our meeting and sat by myself, and had no cause to repent. Desires were felt to be under the influence of that power, which can enable to do or to suffer whatever is best for me; but this is hard to flesh and blood; what need we have to seek Him who alone remains to be the helper of the needy!

In the beginning of the 7th mo. I received the affecting information of the death of my only surviving son, which occurred in a foreign country, after an absence of twelve years. Though consoled with the hope that his long affliction had been sanctified to him, and that he had been mercifully removed from the evil to come, I felt this bereavement an addition to the tribulations which have befallen me.

What a comfort to be favoured with an evidence that our election is made sure! Yet even to those who arrive at this state of being in Him who is the elect, the evidence of it may be withheld, and doubts at times may continue to assail them: nevertheless "the foundation of God standeth sure, having this seal, the Lord knoweth them that are his."

12th mo. 14th. Our Monthly Meeting: the select meeting, the evening before, was a time of refreshment. The words of the Psalmist were brought to my mind, "The Lord preserveth the simple; I was brought low and He helped me." We were favoured with the company of two devoted travellers in the good cause, whose solid example was strengthening to some of us, whose hands often hang down, and knees smite together. Oh! for a mind more redeemed from these lower enjoyments, and an entire subjection to the will of my heavenly Father in all things? I hope I shall not complain, nor think my sufferings hard. I am mortal, and must decay as to the outward, but I am at times comforted (though at others much discouraged) in a hope that the inward man gains a little strength; more however is necessary to come to a certainty of being prepared for admittance into heaven when the spirit leaves this mortal tabernacle.

19th. O my soul! what an awful situation thou

art placed in! Mayst thou be so attentive to the voice of Him that speakest from heaven, that nothing may hinder thy sacred duty to thy God.

12th mo. 29th. We had the company of —— and ——, who were engaged in visiting part of the families of this Monthly Meeting. They seemed low and deeply exercised. How acceptable, in the Lord's time, are the returns of a renewal of strength; and when in mercy this is vouchsafed, what a consolation doth it afford that, as a father pitieth his children, so doth the Lord pity those who love and serve Him. My mind was depressed, I longed to sit, as Mary did, at the feet of a blessed Redeemer.

[Extract of a Letter.]

To a Friend.

Ashford, 2nd mo. 15th, 1831.

My Dear Friend,

I have been looking at the date of thy affectionate letter; I remember it raised a feeling in my heart then that did me good, and the same is revived again. But how soon do these tender impressions like a shadow pass away! Every state seems to require steady watchfulness, and how difficult to keep to. This morning at meeting, I thought we were favoured to feel real refreshment, a little heavenly dew which replenished my feeble mind. I returned better than I went, and it afforded some hope of being fed again in the afternoon. But O, how different! how has my mind been wandering before I was aware, forgetting the solemn occasion for which we were met. But the

good remembrancer is ever watching over us for good;
the arm of His tender mercy is stretched out still, to
bring such wanderers back through painful returning
steps, and to direct safely to His fold of everlasting
rest, all those who are devoted faithfully to follow
Him, and whose hearts are entirely given up and
willing to be counted by all men as fools for His sake.
It is this renunciation of every selfish will, a becoming
like passive clay, I long to experience; then I do
believe hard things will be made easy, and resignation given to follow the Lamb whithersoever he is
pleased to lead, though it may be through many
tribulations and deep provings. I often feel as though
my end was near. I never felt greater need of watchfulness, and fear lest I fall a prey to a cruel enemy,
and be at last taken captive at his will—never more
need of the prayers of my friends, than now in my
feeble old age, not able to help myself to one good
thought. I hope, dear friend, when thou art favoured
sensibly to draw near the source of all good, thou
wilt not forget thy exercised friend; and be en-
couraged to do what thy hands find to do with all thy
might; remember that whilst health and strength are
afforded is the most acceptable time for service.

Thy affectionate friend,

M. H.

3rd mo. 4th, 1831. Through unwatchfulness and
inattention to that which alone leads safely, I was as
one left to myself—one that had no anchor, nothing
to stay myself upon, tossed as with a tempest,

and not comforted : but striving to wait quietly, I felt an impulse to fall on my knees, and mentally pray to Him who seeth in secret, and heareth prayer, that I might know the strong man cast out, and all his goods spoiled. My dear children too were brought near my heart with strong breathings, that He who maketh the clouds his chariot, and walketh upon the wings of the wind, might be pleased to protect and guide them safely to his holy mountain, and make them joyful in his house of prayer.

6th. We had the Yearly Meetings' Committee at Ashford preparative meeting; though they were not large in testimony, yet they had a word in season. May it prove as a dew from the Lord, as the showers upon the grass, that tarry not for man, nor wait for the sons of men.

5th mo. Every dispensation of Divine Providence calls loudly on us to pray always, and in every thing to give thanks; but how hard is this to attain.

6th mo. 19th. I attended the funeral of our valued cousin, M. I., at Colne; her illness was long and very suffering; she was enabled to bear it with patience and resignation. She dropped some weighty expressions, to the comfort and consolation of her afflicted husband. She said her spirit was sweetly at rest in Jesus, the sting of death was taken away, and the grave would have no victory over her, &c. &c. It was a day to be remembered with humble gratitude; a very precious covering came over us in the meeting, and particularly at the grave side, where dear William kneeled by his most valued earthly treasure, and reverently acknowledged the support of the everlasting Arm; he craved that the blessing of resignation might still be granted. After tea several testimonies were borne.

The goodness and tender mercies of Israel's Shepherd was enforced, and that the Lord was a strong-hold in the day of trouble. I felt very unworthy to partake with my friends and many relations, of a few crumbs of heavenly bread, at such a time of solemnity. O my soul, bless thou the Lord, and forget not all his benefits; for though he is pleased often to try thee with deep poverty, he seeth the way that thou takest, and as thou trusteth in him, he will prove himself a present helper when vain is the help of man.

After this I went to Coggeshall, Kelvedon, and Chelmsford, and returned to Ashford the 20th of 7th month, where I found my son and daughter and their child well. All thanks belong to the bountiful Giver of every good. Oh! that heavenly things may ever be the primary object of my pursuit.

8th mo. 9th. When I first sat down in our evening meeting, the inability and weakness of my poor feeble tabernacle seemed to weigh me down, nor did I strive enough to get to the place of true waiting, for which I felt pain of heart. It is a mercy that the rod is permitted, and we kept on the watch, especially in meetings. We read that when " the sons of God presented themselves before the Lord, Satan presented himself also;" and this is still no doubt known to be the case, by those who are endeavouring to approach the sacred footstool with acceptance; for there is nothing that the enemy of our souls strikes at more, and endeavours to destroy, than the precious life. How needful then to maintain the watch, and resist him, stedfast in the faith, remembering the encouraging promise, " Because thou hast kept the word of my patience, I also will keep thee from the hour of temptation." Happy experience! cleave close, O my soul! to thy Saviour, and wait daily upon him for strength to step along safely, through the wilderness of this world, to a house not made with hands, eternal in the heavens.

18th. We had a very acceptable visit from S. G., and —— engaged in a visit to the county. The public meeting here was small, on account of the very short notice, but satisfactory. When thus reached by the renewed visitation of our heavenly Father's love, we feel fervent in desire to be strengthened to follow the Captain of our salvation. But how weak are our resolutions, unless divinely assisted by that faith which Truth inspires!

9th mo. 12th. Dover monthly meeting was small but comfortable; it was owned by Him who is the beloved of souls. Whom have we in heaven but Thee? and there is none upon earth that we desire in comparison of Thee?

19th. I went to the Quarterly Meeting at Maidstone, where we had the company of C. H., from America, and ——, and ——, with certificates—pillars in the house of our God, faithful watchmen on the walls of our Sion.

10th mo. 13th. At Folkstone meeting I was favoured

to feel a degree of that love that enlargeth the heart, earnestly desiring ability to give up without reserve to Him who is pleased, at seasons, to give power to the faint, and to those who have no might he increaseth strength.

11th mo. 3rd. Monthly Meeting at Canterbury. At this meeting I believed it my place to inform Friends, that I had felt for many years a concern to pay a religious visit to Friends in Bedfordshire and Hertfordshire, and the families in the compass of Hertford Monthly Meeting. What a prospect for such a poor worm! The meeting entered into feeling with me, and expressed much sympathy. A certificate was directed to be prepared, which was produced and signed at an adjournment of the meeting held at Dover.

12th mo. 2nd. I left Ashford, and was at Hertford Monthly Meeting on the 7th. Oh! that the only safe Director may be with me, keep me little, low, and in his fear, and preserve me from going before the light of his countenance, or so far loitering behind as to lose a sense of it.

On fourth day afternoon, I sat with one family, and went to Hodsdon meeting on fifth day, which was small; but I was sensible of a precious feeling of our heavenly Father's love. Sixth day, returned to Hertford. On First day some pantings for life, I believe, were felt by many, Oh! the want of deeply experienced labourers such as Special West, Mary Pryor, and Samuel Scott, amongst them. The fourth day meeting was a comfortable time. We went that afternoon to

Ware, and attended meeting there on fifth day, which
was small and heavy; how few are willing to leave
behind the hindering things of time, and with firm
resolution to enlist under the banner of truth, and fight
the Lord's battles in his own strength and under his
own direction., May he be pleased to raise up amongst
us judges as at the first, and counsellors as at the beginning! Sixth day I was at Royston meeting in the
evening, it was small, yet He who ever regardeth the
poor and simple was near, blessed be his name! The
First day following at Ashwell, where there are only
three women members of our Society. A Committee
from Hitchin are appointed to attend, three of whom
were present; and I thought we were enabled to labour
in some degree, in the vineyard, and received the
penny. Second day Hitchin, select meeting in the
evening, Quarterly Meeting the next day, the 20th, I
hope I felt thankful in the enjoyment of a quiet silence
in both these meetings. I was also at their fifth day
meeting, and on sixth day was at Luton meeting. Here
I had an accident, so that I could not proceed, but
went to my daughter's at Tottenham. After resting
there about three weeks, I was so far recovered as to
be able to go to Albans, about the 18th of 1st mo.
1832, where there is no meeting, but a few Friends
who seemed pleased to sit down with me, and wait on
Him whose tender mercies are over all his works.
Next day to Hempstead, the next First day, we were at
Ampthill morning and afternoon meetings; the Great
Caretaker owned us; I desire never to forget His
adorable condescension and tender love, which is re-

newed every morning. We were very kindly entertained at ————'s, an agreeable well ordered family,
and spent the evening in a degree of sweet solemnity.
Next day were at Crinfield meeting, and sat with the
few friends there. May they be preserved in a humble
teachable state, and then they will be fed with a few
crumbs, while the rich and the full are sent empty
away.

Went that evening to Newport Pagnell, and returned home with a peaceful mind. To those who are
strong, it would seem small, but of great magnitude
to me, and very comforting. My spirit exclaims,
" What shall I render to the Lord for all his benefits ? " He who made us, knoweth our frame, and remembereth that we are dust, and have nothing of our
own ; and though it was my lot to travail deep before
the spring arose, the great I AM still manifested his
power, and in some degree magnified his own Name.
This Name is precious to a few, and those who truly
gather thereto find it a place of safety.

It is however sorrowful to feel lukewarmness and
indifferency prevail amongst a people that have been
favoured as this people. When in my late engagement,
after sitting in families, I often felt my peace to flow
as a river, as I strove to keep inward and quiet. I
was instructed by a caution in a dear friend's letter,
wherein he said, " Keep thy mind to the exercise of
the day, and be not anxious for the morrow ;" and
that he thought there was much in that part of our
Lord's prayer, as to spirituals, as well as to temporals,
" Give us this day our daily bread." I trust this

advice was a help to me, and I have often wished
our dear exercised brethren would not withhold such
cautions, how often might they help poor travellers on
their way.

2nd mo., 1832. Gave up my certificate at a Monthly
Meeting at Dover, and enjoyed a peaceful mind.

2nd mo. 15th., 1832. At our little week-day meeting, I thought we experienced the precious effects of a
joint, heartfelt labour, in seeking the quickening influence of the true Shepherd, to him the porter openeth,
and the sheep hear his voice ; he calleth his own sheep
by name, and he leadeth them out ; and when he
putteth forth, attention to his inspeaking voice would
lead us into a watchful state of mind, similar to that
of the Prophet, when he said, " I will stand upon my
watch, and set me on the tower, and will watch to see
what He shall say unto me, and what I shall answer
when I am reproved."

In the days of my youth, I have many times thought,
let the poor body suffer whatever it may please Providence to permit, I could bear it, to obtain an unshaken
hope of a resting place at last ; but now age and many
infirmities are come upon me, I find my resolutions
very weak, and that I greatly need best assistance.

4th mo. 28th. This day I heard of the decease of
E. Rickman, wife of our beloved and ancient Friend,
W. Rickman. She filled the office of elder many
years, the loss of such is affecting at so low a time,
when many, as well as the priests—the ministers of
the Lord—weep as between the porch and the altar,
and say, " Spare thy people, O Lord ! and give not

c

thine heritage to reproach, that the heathen should rule over them. Wherefore should they say among the people, where is their God ? "

5th mo. 3rd. Reading the journals of our Friends, and considering their close exercises, often tenders my heart, and leads me to pray for my own preservation and faithfulness, with that of my dear children, who justly claim the first place in my solicitude. My desire is, O Lord! that thou mayst keep them faithful, and in thy fear. Thy wisdom and thy judgments are unsearchable, and thy ways past finding out, and happy are they who move at thy command, and stand stedfast in thy counsel.

10th. Our Monthly Meeting was held at Ashford, and proved a favoured opportunity. A few of its solid members experienced a little life to circulate from vessel to vessel, it was " never said to Jacob's wrestling seed, seek ye my face in vain."

20th, First day. I was at Tottenham meeting, C. O. from America was there, and instructively opened to us the parable of the virgins; those that had been entrusted with the five talents, and had been careful to improve them, had nothing to spare. I believe many were sensible of a precious covering. I was poorly, and did not go to London till sixth day, when I went to Devonshire House, a large gathering ; and I trust that He who was known to His disciples by the breaking of bread, was near. C. H. and C. O. were there, and both appeared in solemn testimony ; but it is affecting to observe the want of tenderness in us. How needful to know the fallow ground of the heart frequently broken up! The following First day, at Newington meeting, that faithful servant of the Most High, S. G. laboured fervently. The hoary head is a crown of glory, if it be found in the way of righteousness.

6th mo. 12th. I left my dear children, and reached Margate to attend our Monthly Meeting, where I hope I endeavoured to do the little faithfully, no time for slothfulness in the vineyard. I went to Dover to the select meeting on second day, and Quarterly Meeting next day, at which our Friend —— attended, who was remarkably led to speak of the unfaithfulness of those who drew back, and desired to be excused, several times repeating the words, "I pray thee have me excused." He advised that such should not continue to resist the call, nor the light they were favoured with : he believed they had not a day nor an hour to spare, and that if such a disposition were persisted in, spiritual death would be the end. How the language sunk into my heart! I longed that we might be humbly waiting to have our strength renewed, obey the gracious call, and unite with those who have come out of great tribulation, and have washed their robes and made them white in the blood of the Lamb, therefore, are they before the throne of God, and serve Him day and night in his temple.

7th mo. 1st. A digging time this afternoon at meeting. Towards the close, I was repaid with a little water of that river which maketh glad the whole heritage of God. Surely he is good to Israel, to all those who seek him with an upright heart. If we are not carefully on the watch, but suffer our minds to be agitated, our dependence becomes diverted by little and little, from the true centre and place of safety, where perfect peace is experienced, though the world and all around us speak trouble. Such as have this dependence, will know it to be a truth fulfilled in their experience, that "They that trust in the Lord shall be as mount Sion, which cannot be removed but abideth for ever."

7th mo. 11th. Was our Monthly Meeting at Dover. I felt it my duty to inform my Friends of an impression of love I had long felt, to visit the meetings of Friends in Nottinghamshire, and a few meetings in going and returning; and requested them to leave the certificate open to visit families at Nottingham, if way should open. Friends expressed their feeling, and made an appointment in order for my liberation to pursue my prospect, and, through adorable condescension, I felt greatly relieved. I had had a view to this engagement for some years, till it became a burden too heavy to bear. Oh! how humbling is the retrospect, I long for more perfect reliance on Him who is still saying, "not by might, or by power, but by my Spirit" is the work to be accomplished; that no flesh should glory in His presence. The great Apostle says, He has chosen the foolish things, to confound the wisdom of this world, and things which are not, to bring to nought things which are. How has the accuser of the brethren been permitted to come in as a flood, and cause a close conflict; but thy mercy, O God! faileth not: be pleased still to lift up a standard against

him, drive him from my dwelling, and spoil all his
goods.

8th mo. 16th. The prospect of leaving home and
being so far separated from my near and dear connexions, at so perilous a time, (the cholera spreading
in London and its neighbourhood) is affecting, but
our blessed Redeemer said, " He that loveth father
or mother, more than me, is not worthy of me ; he
that loveth sons or daughters more than me, is not
worthy of me." " Lord, thou knowest that I love
thee ; " be pleased to increase my love, that so, loving
Thee with all my heart, I may love, with a more
perfect love, thy whole creation for thy sake. Thou
hast bowed my heart this day in a renewed feeling of
thy unmerited goodness. Be pleased to bless my
dear and tender children, by preserving them in thy
holy fear ; cause them to remember thy tender dealings,
thy mercy and thy blessings bestowed from day to
day, and from year to year, sanctify them all, and
give us thankful hearts.

8th mo. 21st. I left London, and arrived at Dun-
stable, the next day at Northampton, and attended
their meeting on fifth day. Mourning and sackcloth
was my lot. I had lost my beloved, my stay and my
staff. I endeavoured to seek him, but I found him
not. I hung my harp upon the willow, and wept
when I remembered Sion. I longed to feel the sweetness of mind, I felt after I had requested the certificate.
On First day, in the afternoon, two tender Friends
called and sat with me, I began to rise a little by their
sympathy, and by an affectionate letter one of them

put into my hand. I often wish our feeling elders
would not withhold little offerings of duty when com-
mitted to their charge, it sometimes proves a balm,
like oil and wine that heals the wound. I believe this
proving dispensation was of infinite service, by shew-
ing the necessity of carefully endeavouring to keep to
the root the precious seed, the only safe Director. He in
tender mercy remembered me, when I had no strength
to crave His help, in a strange land, He spared and
shewed mercy, and put it into the hearts of two pillars
in the church to accompany me in turns to most
families, and all that attend meetings. I thought to
leave a poor elderly Friend who resided several miles
out of town, as no way offered to go, but on looking at
it, I believed condemnation would be my painful feeling, if I passed without seeing her: we went, and the
dear woman was pleased to see her friends in her humble cottage, and we were preciously refreshed by the
tender influences of our heavenly Father's love. Oh!
how is His gathering arm stretched out still. After
this, we spent two nights with our kind attendants, an
elder worthy of double honour, and his valuable
family. Then left them with a peaceful mind, reached
Loughborough, and spent the evening agreeably with
the only Friend's family in that place. Next day went
to Leicester meeting; it was a poor low time. The
First day following, was at Olney meeting, which was
small, but owned by the enriching presence of Him
whose name is holy.

16th. Went to Leighton Buzzard, and spent a
short time with dear ————, whom I had known

many years, and was comforted in her company, she
being a mother in Israel, an elder worthy of double
honour, fresh and green in old age, a beautiful situation. After calling on several other Friends to satisfaction, I returned to Woburn, next day attended
Hoystyend meeting, an old house, where many of our
zealous ancestors had met, and at which place they
were buried. A solemn covering clothed us on our
first sitting down, and by abiding under it, we were
favoured with a good meeting, and enabled to acknowledge the goodness of Him who dwelt in the bush
formerly, and it was not consumed. I reached Stoke
Newington in the afternoon. My mind was comforted
and was clothed with sweet peace. On the 17th of
10th mo., I returned my certificate to Folkstone
Monthly Meeting, having cause to hope the small
dedication of my feeble old age will prove an acceptable evening sacrifice. I feel true satisfaction in reflecting on those I have visited, I trust in gospel love.
May the Father of the faithful, in his unmerited goodness, be pleased to lead about and instruct them by
the drawing cords of His love, in the high and holy
way cast up for his ransomed and redeemed children
to walk in.

11th mo. 28th. At our little meeting I had to
lament my own unwatchfulness, suffering my mind to
wander from its true centre, and greatly feared hearing
the alarming voice, " Other vineyards hast thou kept,
but thine own hast thou not kept." I was sensible of
my error, and oh ! I beg, I pray Thee who alone art
the healer of breaches and restorer of paths to walk
in, to correct my many backslidings.

Let not thy hand spare nor thine eye pity, until Thou hast cleansed me from my many propensities to evil, humbled my soul by thy righteous judgments, and made me what thou wouldst have me to be.

11th mo. 29th. Poor and languid both in mind and body. In the evening, I was comforted in reading a few lines in the Annual Monitor. " He hath covered my sins with His mantle." I longed that I might know this greatly favoured state to be mine, and also know, in passing through the wilderness of this world and vale of tears, that there is a rest for the people of God. A blessed privilege! How lamentable that any should slight it.

12th mo. 19th. I was informed of the decease of ———, of ——, a healthy-looking young man, taken from time, after an illness of about two weeks. He appeared to be mercifully preserved, calm, and composed, though much humbled by a sense of his awful condition, and said he felt willing to be placed amongst the meanest of the Lord's people, if he might but live in His presence for ever. This makes the fifth funeral from his family within about one year and ten months. How alarmingly solemn is the reflection, that every age is liable to the awful stroke, nothing so uncertain as life, or certain as death. Oh! that we may be wise, that we may consider our latter end!

31st. What progress have I made in the heavenly race? Have I not renewed cause to acknowledge that to me belongs blushing and confusion of face? Yet, through abundant condescension, I have been strengthened to make some sacrifices that have felt as

near as that of parting with a right hand or a right
eye, and in giving up to these I feel thankful, that
through the help of Him who hath his way in the
whirlwind and in the storm, and the clouds are the
dust of his feet, I can set up my Ebenezer and say,
" Hitherto hath the Lord helped me." Blessed be his
holy name!

1st mo. 8th, 1833. A precious meeting this morning. My soul was measurably prostrated before the
great I am, under a deep sense of my own unworthiness; and in boundless love, he was pleased to lift up
the light of his glorious countenance upon me, a poor
worm, and I trust that the two or three also, that were
labouring together in His name, were favoured with
the same experience. I said in my heart, oh! that all
the few members in this place would come to a firm
resolution, to leave behind the hindering things of
time, and dedicate two hours to a week-day meeting;
surely they would be strengthened, and enabled from
experience to acknowledge, that one hour in the
Lord's presence is better than a thousand elsewhere.

13th. A sweetly refreshing time at meeting this
morning. The parable of the sower represented by
our dear Saviour, affected my mind. The seed was
sown in four sorts of ground, and but one of these
brought forth fruit to perfection. I longed that we
might know the operation of the separating hand, to
break down and destroy all that offends and obstructs
the work going forward. Some of us, at times, rejoice
in the evidence that we are not following cunningly
devised fables, but the pure, living, eternal substance.

c 3

1st mo. 20th. Although I sat down in meeting this morning in a degree of freshness, and strove to wait in the quiet, I seemed to wait in vain. Entering too freely into needless conversation with a person who came in last evening, was brought to my mind as a charge against me. Oh! my soul, when wilt thou learn to watch the door of thy lips, that thou sin not with thy tongue, and keep thy mouth as with a bridle! He who is infinite in holiness, will not accept an unsanctified offering. It is the righteous that shall hold on their way, and those of clean hands grow stronger and stronger.

2nd mo. 8th. Whilst sitting alone this day, my mind was led to press after heavenly treasure, which alone can truly enrich, and is not subject to decay. Oh! the excellency of divine love. It transcends even the most refined delights of this world; ancient, yet ever new. May I dwell under its holy, sweetening, preserving influence!

19th. Oh! how have I desired this day to be preserved little, low and humble, and to be strengthened to go in and out before this little company, so as to give no cause of offence or stumbling. " Search me, O God! and know my heart, prove me and know my thoughts, and see if there be any wicked way in me, and lead me in the way everlasting. Thou compassest my path and my lying down, and art acquainted with all my ways : for there is not a word in my tongue, but thou, Lord, knowest it altogether."

2nd mo. 24th. The fore part of the meeting this morning was exercising; but striving quietly to wait, we were enabled to draw nigh, the cloud dispersed and a little true light gladdened our hearts : all praise to Him who feedeth the hungry, and thirsty souls with food convenient for them.

25th. On awaking this morning, I was favoured to feel no condemnation, but a sense of gratitude for unmerited mercies. Those who know anything of the operation of true religion on the mind, know that the inward life, which is hid with Christ in God, can only be supported and kept alive by that daily bread which cometh down from heaven ; it is this alone that can nourish the soul on to eternal life. I long to experience this happy state, but it is often my lot to water my pillow with my tears, while I feel similar to the poor publican, who smote upon his breast and said, " God be merciful to me a sinner."

3rd mo. 17th. A very trying meeting this morning, great weakness both of mind and body. Oh that the hand of the dear Redeemer might not spare, nor his eye pity, until the whip of small cords hath done its office, and driven all the buyers and sellers out of the temple of my heart, and made it a fit habitation for Him who is holy, to dwell in.

20th. As I returned from the Quarterly Meeting at Rochester, I was contemplating, with renewed gratitude to a bountiful Creator, how tenderly his Spirit had visited my soul in early life. His appearance at first was small, as a grain of mustard seed ; he inclined my heart to prize it, and, as I grew older, I valued his tender impressions as my chief joy. I have not words to express the thankfulness I have often felt

that I was made so far sensible of the sweet influences
of Divine love—that in middle life, when permitted
from various causes to pass through many tribulations
and besetments, I often walked by myself and strewed
my tears, looking round to see if any one was near to
hear my sighs.   Oh! what cause have I to reflect on
his boundless goodness to the most unworthy that
ever desired to serve him.   He has indeed proved
himself to be in his holy habitation, a Husband to the
widow, and a Father to the fatherless.   He has also
increased my store inwardly and outwardly, and in
my infirm old age, given me to see the greatest
privilege I was ever favoured with, that of his in-
clining my heart to love him and his appearance,
before the days came when I might say, I had no
pleasure in them; giving me to know that I had a
stronghold, a never-failing support, whereto I could
flee in times of trouble.   Oh! that I could continually
rest here till death is swallowed up of victory.

3rd mo. 24th. A humbling season to those to
whom the Holy Name is precious.   Those who
gather to this Name find a place of safety.

5th mo. 1st. On our sitting down in meeting, a
sweet solemnity covered my mind.   In the afternoon,
I called to see a neighbour who was ill, and in conversation I said more than became me; and when I
lay on the pillow at night, reflecting how the day
had been spent, confusion and distress became my
just portion.   I had not watched the door of my
lips, but had sinned with my tongue.   This scripture
seemed fulfilled in my experience, " Man's heart is

deceitful above all things, and desperately wicked, who can know it? I the Lord search the heart, I try the reins." There is mercy with the Lord that He may be feared. I went to my neighbour, and acknowledged my fault. It seemed to her a light matter, but I had peace in yielding, though it was humbling to me. I feel utterly unworthy of the least notice of my Father who is in heaven, and crave for strength to bow at His sacred footstool, that he would renewedly manifest his power, and sit as a refiner and purifier of silver, that so an offering might be made to Him in righteousness.

27th. I was at Tottenham, in which place, in years that are over and gone, I had to wade through many discouragements. Such reflections too much prevailed this morning; in the afternoon, through unutterable condescension, divine help overcame depression, and I left the meeting with a peaceful mind.

29th. I went to see a relation in declining health, who appeared to be sinking fast as to the body, but I trust she was under the pruning hand of Him who doeth all things well, and that He is preparing her by the workings of His own good Spirit for a place in His kingdom, where no unclean thing can ever enter.

6th mo. 1st. I attended a sitting of the Select Meeting, and I hope I was favoured to feel, in some degree, the very great privilege of collecting with my Friends, and endeavouring to gather a few crumbs that fell from the table.

4th. I went to Hertford to visit my nephew, and

was at their meeting to satisfaction. The remembrance of the many pleasant hours I spent on these
premises, with my husband and little family, when I
felt the gathering arm of everlasting love tendering my
heart, and enabling me to make solemn covenant with
the God of my youth, the renewed feeling of this His
goodness humbled my mind this day, even to tears;
and fervent breathings of soul were raised within me,
that the outstretched arm of tender compassion might
be still · extended, to draw the wanderers to a true
sense of their responsible situation, deeply to ponder
their ways, and remember that " it is not in man that
walketh to direct his steps," but " a good man's ways
are ordered of the Lord."

6th mo. 14th.   I returned to Ashford, and felt
thankful to sit down in our comfortable little meeting
on the 16th.

17th.   I went to Dover, and attended the Select
Meeting.   I felt poor and stripped; but after sitting
some time, Divine Love was· pleased to humble my
heart, whereby I was made willing to take my
part of the exercise of the day, as conveyed by the
answers to the queries; the consideration of which
raised a desire that my own heart might be stirred
up, so to labour, so to be rooted and grounded in
the love of Truth, and the knowledge of the Gospel
of Christ, that no temptation on the one hand or on
the other, might shake me in these dreadful shaking
and trying times, when the Lord may search Jerusalem as with candles, which search is for the
punishment of those who are settled on their lees.

18th. I attended the Quarterly Meeting, towards the close of which, the stone seemed rolled from the well's mouth, whereby the spring was permitted to arise and refresh the seed. It was said by the Angel to Mary, " The Lord God shall give unto Him the throne of his father David, and he shall reign over the house of Jacob for ever, and of his kingdom there shall be no end."

7th mo. 10th. That beautiful Psalm, the 23rd., was sweetly brought to my mind on first waking, " The Lord is my Shepherd I shall not want, he maketh me to lie down in green pastures, he leadeth me beside the still waters, he restoreth my soul, he leadeth me in paths of righteousness for his name's sake; yea, though I walk through the valley of the shadow of death, I will fear no evil, for thou art with me; thy rod and thy staff they comfort me. Thou preparest a table before me in the presence of mine enemies; thou anointest my head with oil, my cup runneth over. Surely goodness and mercy shall follow me all the days of my life, and I will dwell in the house of the Lord for ever." This proved to me a memorable and humbling day. I was in ill health, and had thought of giving up going to sit with the few at our little meeting. How many are bowed down in this day of trial, under fear of falling as by the hand of Saul their enemy, yet at times do we not feel strength to acknowledge, " Hitherto has the Lord helped us :" his reward is precious indeed for every little act of obedience.

7th mo. 15th. My heart was affected on my

pillow with these words, " Eye hath not seen, nor ear heard, neither hath it entered into the heart of man to conceive the good things that God hath in store for them that love Him." What can poor finite man do ? his natural comprehension cannot enter into the mysteries of the things that belong to Christ's kingdom, for they are spiritually discerned. Oh ! that every traveller Sion-ward, with my own soul, may daily witness the everlasting covenant of life and peace, even the sure mercies of David.

16th. Low and tried with bodily weakness, in the afternoon more lively. How instructive are such changes, Do they not evince that the manna gathered yesterday will not sustain to-day ? it must be laboured for every day : I desire to remember this.

8th mo. 3rd. On sitting down to my comfortable, yet frugal meal, my heart was tenderly affected with the manner in which that bountiful hand that provides for the sparrows has provided for me all my life long. O my soul, mayst thou live in His fear and love his law !

[Extract of a letter.]
Ashford, 27th of 8th mo., 1833.

MY DEAR FRIEND,

I think I should be very ungrateful if I did not feel obliged for thy kind sympathy, I believe true faith that worketh by love gradually cleanseth the heart, and causeth a near affection to flow towards those who are often bowed with earnest desire to be brought into a humbling sense of their own inability

even to think a good thought. Who so poor as the
Lord's servants, and stript as his messengers—for
this reason, because in a religious sense they have
nothing of their own, and what is given as apprehended duty is so small and simple, and they feel so
foolish in the exercise, they are ready to start aside
like broken bows? Thou knowst, dear friend, that
for all these small acts of dedication the reward is
sure with Him that cannot err, but is often choosing
the weak and simple things of this world to confound
the wise, and things that are not to bring to nought
things that are, that our dependence may be entirely
fixed on our heavenly Father, and centred in his
love. This feels a very favoured state, and in it no
flesh can glory in his presence. I do not know how
I came to write on such an important subject, but
have been musing by myself, and it is just what
came before me. Remember the blessing that is
attached to the poor in spirit, and watch against
getting too low. This is a day in which we are
loudly called upon to watch and pray, that the eye
may be opened in us that can discover the assaults
of a cruel enemy; he will, if possible, bring those
he cannot raise up into a heavy, depressed, dejected
situation of mind, which is very trying to bear,
and will not forward our religious growth. In the
prophet's days, " Jerusalem was to be searched with
candles, which searching was for the punishment of
those that were settled on their lees." Is not the
present an awakening day? I have desired it might
prove so to my poor mind, that has been too much

inclined to ease and indifference. But now surely
there is cause to feel and mourn for our desolation.
This Quarterly Meeting has its trials, and feels its
weakness, that we had need to put on strength, and
wait on Him who is alone able to renew it, and
by our example and precept exalt his ever adorable
Name. He can speak peace when trouble surrounds
us on the right hand and on the left—the promise
is to the mourners that they shall be comforted.

Thy affectionate friend,

M. H.

10th mo. 16th. Our valued friend, W. Rickman
attended our Particular Meeting, and revived the
inquiry, " Is there no balm in Gilead, is there no
Physician there ? Why then is not the health of the
daughter of my people recovered ? " and very instructively mentioned the visitations of his youth,
which from an experienced Friend, who had attained
the eighty-eighth year of his age, seemed like a cup
of cold water to one who was ready to faint.

10th mo. 27th. How busy was the tempter this
morning, besetting my mind with many wandering
thoughts, to draw from the true Source of adoration
and worship, surely if the Lord were the chiefest of
ten thousand and altogether lovely, my distress would
not be so great; but a death-like insensibility too
much prevails over me. Oh! that in my old age, I
might know more than ever the cleansing operation
of the Spirit, to purify, not only from the drossa nd
the tin, but also from the reprobate silver ; and that

thus I might know his rod and his staff to comfort me.

30th. I long to be more deeply humbled under a sense of my own unworthiness. The valley is sweet to dwell in, but my poor mind is often comparable to the mountains of Gilboa, where there is neither rain, nor dew, nor fields of offering.

11th mo. 10th. We had the excellent advices of the Yearly Meeting read, I was ready to say in my heart, what can be done 'that is not done? Our little Society.has been from the beginning as a garden enclosed by our wholesome discipline; but how have we slept whilst the enemy has made great encroachments, and broken down our wall in many instances, and caused the living to go heavily on their way. The Spirit of a suffering Lord in the hearts of his people leads to an inward exercise for the salvation of mankind. Thus when we behold a visited people, entangled by the things of this world, and thereby rendered incapable of being faithful examples to others, sorrow and heaviness, is often experienced; and so, in measure, is filled up that which remains of the sufferings of Christ. Can our hearts endure or our hands be strong, if we desert a cause so precious, if we turn away from a work in which so many have patiently laboured.

20th. Our week-day meeting was better attended than usual. My bodily infirmities had a powerful effect on my mind, and I had to lament the insensible state I sat in, having little strength to labour. I remembered in the afternoon the dear Redeemer's deep

suffering, when he prayed thus, Oh ! my Father, if it
be possible, let this cup pass from me; " but in this he
centred, " Not my will, but Thine be done." When
he returned from prayer, he found his disciples sleep-
ing, and said, " What, could ye not watch with me one
hour ? " The consideration affected and humbled my
mind. I do not expect it will be long before the
narrow confines of the silent grave will enclose me.
Oh ! happy moment, if I may, in unutterable mercy,
when freed from the many struggles and conflicts of
time, soar above, where nothing can annoy. Remember then, Oh ! my soul, the necessity of living in
the fear and dread of thy Creator, and that thou must
be washed, cleansed, and sanctified.

12th mo. 3rd. I believed duty required me to pay
a visit to a young man sinking to the grave in a decline.
However simple these requirings appear to those not
of our Society, I went much in the cross, but had the
evidence of peace in the engagement, and I believe
the presence of Zion's King was felt.

18th. Heard of the death of Mary Alexander of
Kelvedon.   She had been many years a devoted
labourer in the Lord's vineyard. He hath made the
depths of the sea, a way for his ransomed to pass over.
Her Master whom she served was with her, whereby
she was enabled to draw water from the well of
salvation, and to partake of those refreshing streams
of divine consolation that make glad the whole city of
God, and no doubt has triumphantly entered into his
courts with praise.

22nd. Indisposition this day prevented my meeting

in social worship with my friends. I hope I was not altogether unmindful of my duty, and the various testimonies we are called upon to bear. My mind was tenderly affected by remembering, that our holy and merciful High Priest is touched with a feeling of our infirmities. May He incline my heart more firmly to lean upon, and to trust in him.

1st mo. 1st, 1834. Every year and every day brings me nearer the awful time, when a separation must be made from every near and dear connexion, and the silent grave will enclose this earthly tabernacle. Oh! for an increase in humility, faithfulness, and obedience to the revealed will. This is what I pray for, for myself and for my dear children, that we may be strengthened in an unshaken belief in the efficacy of the blood of the beloved Son of God, our Lord and Saviour Jesus Christ, who came down from heaven, and took not on him the nature of Angels, but the seed of Abraham, was born of the Virgin Mary, suffered under Pontius Pilate, the cruel and shameful death of the cross, to be a propitiation for the sins of the whole world; rose again the third day from the dead, and ascended into heaven, and is the advocate and mediator between God and man, the King, High Priest, and Prophet of his Church, the only author of salvation unto all them that obey him, true God and perfect man.

1st mo. 9th. I attended Monthly Meeting at Folkstone, towards the close, a few words impressed my mind; but I was desirous, Gideon like, to try the fleece both wet and dry, and begged to be preserved from [yielding to] a false opening, lest I might bring reproach on the best cause, and distress on my own mind. The second sitting was more relieving. The next day, I called on a few friends, and came home with a thankful heart. I long to become as passive clay in my heavenly Father's hand, moulded and operated upon as he pleaseth; he only knoweth what is convenient for me. Keep me, O Lord, near to thyself, be with me in that awful moment that is approaching, that Death may never be a King of terrors, but a welcome messenger, that thus he may be swallowed up of victory. Thou art, O my God, in truth worthy, worthy of adoration and worship!

1st mo. 12th. We were favoured at meeting this morning with a humbling, quiet waiting, and felt the shadow of the Divine wing sweetly hovering over us. I felt my own weakness, and that I had nothing to return but a fervent breathing in secret to Him who alone can prepare my heart for any impression He may be pleased to stamp upon it; and may it be that of humility and his fear, during my stay in mutability, and afterwards may I be permitted to join the triumphant church in praising the Lord God and the Lamb for ever and ever!

15th. Ill health prevented my joining my Friends in social worship. The work of the enemy is to prevent our frequent resorting to prayer as being presumptuous in us; but have we not the greatest encouragement to approach the footstool of divine mercy? yet let us ever remember that if we regard iniquity in our hearts the Lord will not hear us.

20th. On sitting down in meeting this morning,

Martha's salutation to her sister Mary came comfortably to my mind, "The Master is come, and calleth for thee." It raised an earnest desire that we might be more attentive to this awakening call of the dear Redeemer, to his inspeaking voice, which, if submitted to and followed, would make "the wilderness like Eden, and the desert like the garden of the Lord; joy and gladness would be found therein, thanksgiving and the voice of melody."

26th. By the calm feelings of my mind on returning from Canterbury, I had reason to conclude I had not done wrong by leaving my own little meeting to sit with Friends in that place, we were drawn by the cords of love into sweet silent waiting, in which we were favoured to feel our covenant renewed. "Whereunto we have already attained, let us walk by the same rule, let us mind the same thing."

2nd mo. 2nd. This morning was a preciously favoured meeting. Blessed be the only Head of His own church, whether gathered in a large number, or only the two or three. We had cause to acknowledge that His tender regard doth not fail to the workmanship of His holy hand.

9th. I have had to pass through some proving seasons, from want of more entire resignation to apprehended duty; nevertheless, I hope I have been favoured to know something of the love of God, and in it to be bound in love with the members of the true church, and to know with them something of the unity of the one Spirit, which makes them as epistles written in one another's hearts, which neither time nor distance can ever erase.

23rd. When first I sat down in meeting this morning, the devourer, whom my soul hates, came upon me like a flood; I felt no strength for war, but endeavouring to divest myself of every thought, and breathing to my ever blessed Helper for patience to suffer, after a time of close labour, the intercession with the Father was pleased to arise for my help, and we were comforted together. O my soul, mayst thou dwell low with his seed that is in bondage, that thou mayst be favoured to arise with him who has done much for thee.

12th. Attended the Select Meeting at Canterbury, it was a uniting time, several instructive remarks were made by the Quarterly Meeting's Committee. I desired to treasure up my part; I believe it is with us now, as dear J. Churchman observes, there are some nursing mothers, many forward instructors, but too few fathers in the church. Such are wanting amongst us as are willing to take our beloved young people by the hand, leading them in the way of the blessed cross, endeavouring to protect through dangers and difficulties, that they may be favoured in their tender age to see and feel the beauty, the comfort, and the safety of the leadings of Christ the good Shepherd, who said, " I know my sheep and am known of mine."

23rd. I believe our meeting was comfortably owned by the good Preserver this morning; I earnestly desired to gather up the fragments that remained of our late favoured visit; and that our little company with whom I so often meet, might labour still more after lowliness of heart, serving the Lord in our generation, and one another in his pure fear; that so we may know him to be our rest, and his peace our quiet habitation: then will he feed his, faithful labourers with heavenly bread, and honour them with his life-giving presence.

3rd mo. 30th. Our morning meeting was to me very depressing, and almost lifeless. When He the Lord of life is pleased to withdraw himself from us for a season, how weak we are, and subject to be assailed by our unwearied enemy. But at such seasons, let us endeavour to wait in the quiet, for help to buckle on the armour, and maintain the watch; and oh! that our covering may be the helmet of salvation, the breast-plate of righteousness, and the girdle of truth; and our weapons the shield of faith and the sword of the Spirit, against which the enemy will never be suffered to prevail. In the afternoon, we had cause to thank God, and take courage.

4th mo. 6th. I believe some of our minds were favoured this morning to partake in degree of heavenly dew, that tendered and refreshed our hearts. In the afternoon, a little of the same precious life. In passing through the streets on First days, have often observed my neighbours spending their time in a careless manner, and have felt a secret salutation of love to them, as a seed ungathered. When it shall please the Lord to open their eyes to behold Sion a quiet habitation, I earnestly wish no stumbling-block in us who are making so high a profession, may be suffered to offend beholders, or dim Sion's heavenly beauty.

20th. Some hunger and thirst experienced after the bread of life. May our heavenly Father, whose

D

tender care for his children, far exceeds that of a
natural parent, be pleased to administer bread to the
hungry, and water to the thirsty souls, that they faint
not by the way.

5th mo. 11th.   I enjoyed this evening the privilege
of meeting with my Friends in social worship, after
having been confined three weeks by illness.   I have
endeavoured to consider my past life, and to remember
the sins of my youth; and my iniquities have been
brought feelingly to my remembrance.   The language
of my heart has been, "Pardon my transgressions,
and remember not my sins, for thy mercy's sake, O
Lord! and for my dear Redeemer's sake.   I beg that
every wrong thing in me may be brought to judgment.
Let every high thought and imagination be brought
down, and laid in the dust, and thy great and excellent
name be more and more exalted.

16th.   In looking over my chequered life from my
early years, I have to admire with feelings of reverent
gratitude the many preservations, gracious dealings,
long-suffering, and tender mercies of a bountiful
Creator to myself, who am the most unworthy that
ever desired to serve him.   The greatest of all his
blessings (as I have ever esteemed it, and now in
humble thankfulness I acknowledge it to be so) is,
that he not only visited, but inclined my heart to
cherish his appearances, and made me sensible of the
sweet impressions of his tendering love in seasons of
retirement, like a canopy to cover my mind.   Oh!
my dear children, I entreat you keep close to his
precious light that has often tenderly visited your
minds; it will assuredly be a light to your feet and a

lantern to your path, as it was to David's formerly.
Seek him by night and by day ; give not up wrestling
till you have obtained the blessing of a quiet and
peaceful mind. I have often had cause to believe his
holy ear was open to my cry, and in his fatherly compassion he has not only calmed my distressed mind,
but often raised up friends to my humbling admiration and comfort; that I can say by some degree of
experience, the Lord is a strong-hold in the day of
trouble. Had I not known, unworthy as indeed I
am, this place of safety and rock of defence, I had
long ere now been swallowed up by the waves of temptation. The devourer was permitted to rage with vio-
lence against me; I know him to be a cruel enemy, my
soul hates him, and often craves earnestly for strength
to set a double watch on the weak side, that in my
feeble old age I may escape his envious baits. Oh !
for my endeared sons and daughters, and tender grand-
children ! may that Great Power, who remains to be
a God hearing and answering prayer to all those who
keep their covenant with him—may He preserve you
as in the hollow of his hand—may He condescend in
the riches of his boundless goodness, to protect and preserve you near to himself, while passing through this
thorny wilderness. Wait upon him, dear children, feel
after his strengthening influence, so will he be to you,
as to your tried mother, in many conflicts, a rock sure
and stedfast, a never-failing help, if your hearts are
stayed on him. I have abundant cause, in the fresh
feeling of his tender mercies, to prostrate my soul
before him, and according to my small ability praise
his ever worthy and great name, and to crave that

living cries might ascend to him to bring my tender
connexions on their way, rejoicing in the footsteps of
the flock of the faithful companions of Jesus.

5th mo. 29th. I went to see a relation in ill
health, much reduced. It is according to the gracious purposes of our faithful Creator to bring down
to the brink of the grave, and in mercy to plead with
us, causing us to pass through many baptisms and
searchings of heart, setting our sins in order before
us. I much desire this may be his case, and my own;
and that the Divine hand may not spare, nor His eye
pity, until we are weaned more, far more, from a
delight in the things of this world, and inclined to
seek more earnestly the kingdom of heaven, with
a firm belief that all things needful will be added.

I hope I feel thankful in having been permitted to
attend the greater part of the sittings of this Yearly
Meeting, through the tender regard of an ever watchful Providence, in restoring my health which had
been impaired before I left home. Oh! how every
attack shakes my aged frame, and every day, whether
improved or not, brings me nearer and nearer the
place appointed for all living—the awful separation
must take place, the soul must appear at the bar of
Divine justice. I pray that a humbling sense of this
solemn truth may continually rest on my mind, and
contrite my spirit before Him who gave me a being,
and hath been with me all my life. When I am sensible of his heart-tendering love, I rejoice in His
presence, and am willing to leave all, that I might
possess the lowest place in His glorious kingdom.
But in times of withdrawing, I greatly fear, and long

to feel a more firm reliance on Him who is just and holy; righteousness was the girdle of His loins, and faithfulness the girdle of His reins—no guile was found in Him, He is himself the truth—His soul was filled with tenderness and flowed with love—He wept over Jerusalem, and over the grave of Lazarus—His miracles were works of mercy, of compassion, and of power—He was lowly in heart—He came not to be ministered unto but to minister.

8th mo. 3rd. Close labour at meeting : may the root be kept alive whether any greenness appear or not on the branches. The evening meeting, a tendering and contriting season; how consoling is the evidence, that we are through all and every conflict the subjects of protecting care; and for all who sincerely love Him He *will care*, though He sometimes suffers them, for hidden purposes, to go bowed down with their hands on their loins.

9th. I am this day informed of the death of my dear friend, M. G., of Tottenham ; a character much hid to the world, but in her, observers may behold the example of a true Christian.

22nd. I woke this morning in a quiet serene frame of mind, sensible in some degree of the sweet presence of Him who dwelt in the burning bush formerly, and it' was not consumed : a favour indeed to one so totally unworthy !

30th. Reading J. B.'s Select Anecdotes, my heart was humbled into prayer for myself, my dear children, and my affectionate nieces, who are now my companions, that we might individually unite in exercise, to feel after and cherish the workings of th

Spirit in each of our breasts; it would bring down every high thought and exalted imagination, soften and contrite our spirits, and often melt us into tears. How desirable is the state of those who, by close attention to the still small voice, are permitted sweetly to commune with their Creator: they can acknowledge " when I am weak then am I strong."

31st. First day morning, a trying meeting to me, though more largely attended than usual. It is not the number, but living, faithful labourers, striving reverently to wait at the footstool of Jesus, that they may know those times of refreshment that come from His presence, being in some degree acquainted with the efficacy of that secret influence which is not of us, though in us. In the afternoon, he who sleepeth not by day nor slumbereth by night, according to His loving-kindness remembered us, and comforted those that mourned.

9th mo. 10th. [At meeting.] A dear Friend in a solemn manner said, " the Lord is in his holy temple, let all the earth keep silence before him." Though I am deprived in great measure from hearing, I thought I enjoyed a full recompence by the solemnizing effect; and I desired to be brought into true submission to the Divine will, that so I might be able to abide the day of His coming, and stand when He appeareth, who is as a refiner's fire; for so it must be with those that love and fear Him, that they may offer unto the Lord an offering in righteousness. How great is the harvest, and how few are the faithful labourers! Yet blessed be his name, he has not left himself without a witness, neither is his glory departed. There are those

who can at times say, "how goodly are thy tents,
O Jacob, and thy tabernacles, O Israel; the Lord
our God is with us, and the shout of a king is
amongst us."

25th. My niece went with me to Maidstone, and to
London next day : the idea of spending a while with my
precious children and sweet grand-children, I view with
pleasure, yet with trembling, knowing my own many
weaknesses and liability to turn aside from constant
watchfulness and preserving fear; lest, instead of becoming a waymark to serious inquirers, I should give
cause for stumbling and reproach. Lord, preserve me
and mine from falling on the right hand or on the left,
and be with us in the way that we go! How closely
did our dear Lord and Saviour press the inquiry upon
Peter, " Lovest thou me?" and I think at this season
of renewing my covenant, I can reply as Peter did,
" Lord thou knowest all things, thou knowest that I
love thee." But how many deaths we have to die,
before that life reigns in us that gives the victory over
the world, the flesh, and the devil!

11th mo. 2nd. Before I arose this morning my
heart was visited, and tendered by my heavenly
Father's love, and a degree of confidence raised, that
if I faithfully followed on to know the Lord, his preserving care would be with me the few remaining
moments of my probationary life. What a mercy to
one so totally unworthy, and so near the confines of
the silent grave; may a sense of reverent thankfulness ever rest on my heart, and may a renewed
feeling of Christian love. increase and enlarge, with
near sympathy, not only for my own family and those

of the same community, but for my fellow-creatures the world over. I believe every true Christian, by the power of the gospel working on his mind, must be liberal minded; and I regret sometimes to observe those who are called such, very uncharitable to their brethren who differ from them. Real Christians, or children of God, and sincere followers of the Redeemer, are of one heart and of one soul, wherever scattered, and whatever may be their outward form of religion : these of every nation, kindred, tongue, and people, love one another, and have one common Parent.

29th. I have found it an advantage, as soon as awake in the morning, to endeavour to turn my mind inward, to wait upon God, to feel his good presence, and lift up my heart to him for protection during the day; and in the evening, to look to him, and consider if my conduct has pleased him; and if we are sensible our ways have met with his approbation, how sweetly, under these consoling reflections, do we take our rest in sleep! I was favoured to feel tenderness of heart, tears of contrition flowed freely while reading the first chapter of first Corinthians, "God hath chosen the foolish things of the world to confound the wise, and God hath chosen the weak things of the world to confound the things that are mighty, that no flesh should glory in his presence."

10th mo. 17th. I was affected by hearing of the death of J. D. and M. C., both valuable elders of the same Monthly Meeting; I had the privilege of their acquaintance from early age, and was instructed by their example. They saw the safety of an humble life, took up the cross, and followed a crucified

Saviour. For wise purposes, that we have no right to question, our holy High Priest has seen meet of late, to call many of his labourers from the church militant on earth, to unite to his church triumphant in heaven. Many mourn the stripped state of our Society, few indeed are coming up in their footsteps; nor can we say of many of our sons as formerly, that they are as plants growing up in their youth, or of our daughters, that they are as corner-stones polished after the similitude of a palace!

1835, 1st mo. 2nd. On my pillow the good Remembrancer, in infinite love, tendered my heart by the consideration, of how swiftly my precious time passes! How has the last year been spent? Have I resigned my heart more freely than in former ones, to that Power who justly claims a full surrender? Oh! Lord, keep me low, keep me humble, keep me more—far more attentive to thy divine will, and faithful to all thy requirings, wheresoever thou art pleased to lead—search every corner of my heart, that every secret sin may be purged away by the redeeming power of thy Son; and that I may witness that essentially needful baptism, whereby I can feel a willingness to be accounted a fool for my dear Saviour's sake, who has done so much for me. Good Jacob was humbled, when he acknowledged, " I am not worthy of the least of all thy mercies which thou hast shewed to thy servant, for with my staff I passed over this Jordan, and now I am become two bands."

14th. Through unmerited mercy, I was favoured with a comforting degree of the heavenly presence. Though this suffering frame must moulder and return

D 3

to its mother earth, a secret hope is vouchsafed, that the everlasting arm will be underneath; and I earnestly crave it may strengthen my poor drooping mind to press forward, until I arrive at that city that hath no need of the light of the sun or of the moon to enlighten it, for the Lord God and the Lamb are the light thereof.

22nd. I very much desire to know, more than ever, the operation of the Father's pruning hand, not only lopping off the superfluous branches, but striking at, and destroying the very root of sin, and to experience his woundings to heal, and killings to make alive. By his fatherly chastisement he bringeth us into the near attachment of sons and daughters; and by his righteous judgments, he brings his children into a stedfast reliance on himself. He watereth and feedeth his flock, he sheltereth his lambs, and prepareth a banquet for his chosen, and maketh them sweetly to rest as at noon. Oh! Lord God, thou whose mercies are both ancient and new, I pray thee leave me not nor forsake me, take not thy Holy Spirit from me; give me a heart more fully resigned to follow thee, and do thy revealed will. Be with me in every conflict, let thy presence go with me and guide me through the wilderness of this world, to a house not made with hands, eternal in the heavens. Amen.

24th. I had an impression to call on a friend recovering from ill health, and came home rejoicing that our spirits had been humbled together at the footstool of Grace.

3rd mo. 1st. Dryness and poverty at both meetings, and utter inability to keep myself; yet had some faint desires after good; may the gracious Protector, by his everlasting arm, be felt near at the close of my day, when the shadows of the evening approach.

26th. Sitting down in our little week-day meeting, yesterday, I was enabled to feel the inexpressible privilege that we as a highly professing people, enjoy beyond any others, when we turn our backs on the things of time, and sit down together silently to wait for Divine help to worship and adore that pure holy Being who seeketh to be worshipped in Spirit and in Truth. Oh! that such opportunities were more prized by our beloved young people in particular; and that we might all watch carefully against wandering thoughts, and labour to draw near the Source of all good, that we may be preserved from the snares of the wicked one, who in this day of great excitement, is suiting his baits to our dispositions.

5th mo. 3rd. "Blessed is the man that trusteth in the Lord, and whose hope the Lord is; he shall be as a tree planted by the water, that spreadeth out her roots by the river, and shall not see when heat cometh, but her leaf shall be green; and shall not be careful in the year of drought, neither shall cease from yielding fruit."

8th. In our neighbourhood we have witnessed many loud calls to prepare for our latter end, as Solomon said, " the doors shall be shut in the street, when the sound of the grinding is low, and he shall rise up at the voice of the bird, and all the daughters of music shall be brought low, also when they shall be afraid of that which is high : and fears shall be in the way, and the almond tree shall flourish, and the grasshopper shall be a burden, and desire shall fail, because man goeth to his long home, and the mourners go about the streets."

13th. At our Monthly Meeting held at Ashford, my mind could scarce sustain its weight of exercise, having for a long time a humiliating view of duty required of me, which has often brought me very low, and in my feeble old age, it has been a close concern to feel true resignation. But endeavouring to sink into willingness, I was enabled to cast my burden on my Friends, who feelingly expressed unity, and directed a certificate to be prepared for me to visit the meetings in Essex. I was much relieved, and attended the Yearly Meeting, considering it a renewed mark of my heavenly Father's love, that I could attend many of the sittings ; but I often mused on the important engagement before me, I remembered the stripped tried situation to which David was reduced, and his fearful exclamation, "I shall one day perish by the hand of Saul." Oh! I long that I may more unreservedly obey the voice of the Lord, which is better than sacrifice, and to hearken than the fat of rams. I was much strengthened in this journey by the company of Susannah Brown, of Coggeshall, whose heart an ever watchful Providence inclined to accompany me through the county. The 20th of 6th mo. I went to Chelmsford, where my dear friend S. B. met me ; the 24th, to Witham Monthly Meeting, held at Maldon. I felt much stripped and low, nothing for myself or others, till in a sitting at ——'s, our spirits were replenished by that influence that was better than the increase of corn, wine, or oil. Indeed we were helped to our own admiration, nor have I words to express the tender regard of Him who putteth forth His own, and goeth before them, and at times is pleased to refresh their spirits by leading them beside the still waters; yea, He is causing them to partake of His inexpressible love. We were very kindly conducted from one meeting to another by exercised Friends, whose company was pleasant and edifying; and we were often drawn into silence in their families, which proved a strength to our feeble minds. At S. Grover's, widow of our late valuable Friend, W. Grover, we met with Edward Alexander, from Ireland, with whom we went to Walden. After a meeting in the evening, (appointed on his account,) which proved a silent one, we had a favoured opportunity in ——'s family, dear E. A. was present, my heart was bound in near sympathy for this deeply baptised traveller, which I could not keep to myself: after which his spirit was sweetly humbled in supplication to the God and Father of all our sure mercies, or his exercised aged friend, and which I hope to treasure up as a renewed evidence of my heavenly Father's tender love. Having now finished our visits, I parted with my dear companion, and came to Chelmsford. I stayed their meeting on First day, where I again met dear E. A., who seemed to me like passive clay in the hands of the Great Potter. I was at Tottenham meeting on the 16th of 7th mo.; and after very pleasantly spending a time with my dear children, reached home the 24th, and enjoyed a peaceful mind. " Return unto thy rest, oh! my soul, for the Lord has dealt bountifully with thee."

In days that are past this scripture declaration was often quoted as applicable to our Society, " the people shall dwell alone"—it was when Israel was abiding in his tent, separate from the surrounding nations, that the emphatic exclamation was uttered, " How goodly are thy tents, O Jacob, and thy tabernacles, O Israel! as the valleys are they spread forth, as gardens by the river side, and as cedar trees beside the waters." And of this favoured people, it was declared on the same occasion, " the people shall dwell alone, and shall not be reckoned among the nations."

8th mo. 14th. At the Monthly Meeting at Folkstone, I returned my certificate, and enjoyed a peaceful mind. Oh! my soul, mayst thou ever bow low at the footstool of thy Saviour, and for ever adore and praise his worthy name!

About this time, I received a letter from my late dear companion, S. Brown, informing me of the decease of her beloved sister, Mary Jesup. It might be justly said, she feared the Lord from her youth: I doubt not that the immortal part has taken its flight, to dwell for ever with Him who is Love. Many weighty expressions dropped from her during her illness. " Oh!" said she, " it is so sweet to be quiet, to lie close in the bosom of my Saviour;" many times expressing the peace and comfort she felt. We cannot but mourn the loss of such, whose life and conversation hold forth the language, " follow me, as I have borne the cross, despised the shame, and followed Christ!"

30th. Our morning meeting was to my mind a humbling. season, and in the evening similar, for

which I desire to be thankful. It is utterly impossible
that any thing should bring to the knowledge of the
will of God, but the light and spirit of Christ, by an
inward manifestation.

9th mo. 28th. I went to the London Select Quarterly Meeting, which felt to me a poor, low time. How
precious would the quickening influence of the Holy
Spirit be, as was formerly experienced, when *Truth
reigned over all.* Quarterly Meeting on third day, a
sweet solemnity came over us, by the renewed streams
of that river whose source is everlasting Love.

10th mo. 3rd. Went to Epping; it felt to me like
paying a debt I have owed since I returned from a
visit into Essex. I was enabled to return with my
penny, after calling on all the Friends' families—Oh!
who would not serve so rich a rewarder for so small
an act of obedience!

15th. Folkstone Monthly Meeting—I endeavoured
to draw near the fountain, and returned in possession
of a quiet and easy mind—where little is given, little
is required, neither do we serve a hard Master.

25th. First day, morning and afternoon meetings
were suffering seasons. I long to be made sensible
that I am filling up that part of the sufferings of the
dear Redeemer that is my allotted portion. I had a
pleasant, and I hope, a profitable time of retirement
in the evening, with a young friend that called in.
Such opportunities often afford sweet reflection; and
we are ready to admire that we do not manifest greater
interest in the everlasting welfare of our friends at all
times, and endeavour more, in the social circle, to
edify one another.

11th mo. 8th. A day of heavy conflict in both meetings. What small occurrences disturb and perplex our minds, when Satan, our unwearied enemy, is watching every avenue. Oh! my Father, who art in heaven, and dwellest in the light, be pleased to remember my low estate, and renew my confidence in thy never-failing power. Though I walk through darkness and see no light, oh! stay my drooping mind on thee, and strengthen me to maintain the warfare to the end; for thou remainest to be the strength of the poor, and of the needy in their distress, a refuge from the storm, a shadow from the heat, when the blast of the terrible one is as a storm against the wall!

12th. I attended our Monthly Meeting at Canterbury, where we were remarkably addressed under the influence of best Wisdom. Without this anointing no one can preach the gospel—and if such favoured opportunities are not improved, we shall be accountable at that day, when every talent will be called for at our hands, though it may be but one, and that the smallest of all talents.

In this month, I was visited with illness, which soon brought me very low; I believed it to be a mark of my heavenly Father's love, and a renewed visitation to my soul. I sensibly felt the dear Redeemer's solemn voice, " Steward, give an account of thy stewardship." The impression was weighty and very humiliating for a considerable time: and though I was favoured to feel my mind, in adorable mercy, quiet and easy, and I hope in degree resigned, I could not get to that sweet assurance I earnestly

longed for—and oh! how was a cruel enemy suffered
to buffet me. I strove to wrestle, as Jacob did,
through almost a sleepless night, but strength failed
me, my many holdings back, disobediences, and
omissions of duty, by too much giving way to the
fear of men in days that are long past, were brought
to my afflicted mind with deep and painful anxiety.
After a time of close exercise, and fervent breathing
for help, condescending Goodness was pleased to notice
such a poor worm, and in His tender mercy, to help,
when vain was the help of man. These words almost
constantly rested on my mind for several days, "pray
without ceasing, and in every thing give thanks." This
hard, though necessary reduction of self ought to be a
profitable lesson. I looked on my dear children, who
were all with me, and thought I could freely part
with them, if it were the will of Him who created us;
for I felt his boundless love as a canopy over us, and
that, as they kept close to Him, He would not fail to
protect them in every trial. After a time I began to
amend, and the prospect of returning as to a thorny
wilderness, in which I had experienced many afflicting
seasons, at first, was trying to me; but we cannot
rejoice but through suffering, not abound but through
previous abasement. It is indeed a great blessing,
and well worth every conflict, to be permitted in the
centre of our souls to hold communion with our dear
Saviour. "How excellent is thy loving-kindness, O
God, therefore the children of men put their trust
under the shadow of thy wing." May this'gracious
manifestation of thy love be a lasting benefit to my
mind, and according to thy great mercy, take me and

the tender children thou hast given me; oh! take us under thy holy protecting care. Search and prove us, and do away from our hearts every thought that is opposed to thy righteous government; quicken our resolutions to stand upon our watch, and sit upon the tower, and watch to see what thou wilt say unto us, and what we shall answer when we are reproved. Preserve us, O dearest Father, from all the fiery darts of the wicked one, and give us that faith that is invincible; be thou our refuge and defence while sojourning in the wilderness of time, and passing through Jordan's flood, to Canaan's land. Keep us, I beseech thee, in a feeling sense of thy preserving fear, and from a desire to form for ourselves an easier way to thy pure and holy kingdom than that already made by our perfect Pattern, thy beloved Son, who is the Way, the Truth, and the Life. Oh! Lord my God, enable us, by the workings of thy power, to take up our cross, and serve thee faithfully all the days of our appointed time; and give us an inheritance in thy holy city, that hath no need of the sun nor of the moon to enlighten it, for thy glory does lighten it, and thy Lamb is the light thereof. Amen, and amen, saith my soul.

12th mo. 11th.   During the above illness, in which her recovery appeared doubtful, the following expressions were taken down :—

" I felt very low and poorly in the night, but I had a comfortable hope (though it did not continue long with me) that all would be well, that I am ready to think the time is nearly come."

13th.   Two friends calling to see her, she remarked,

" I have been dwelling as in a dry and thirsty land, and though I have endeavoured to labour through a long life, I have nothing of my own to boast of; and in the evening, on hearing the 10th verse of the 37th Psalm, " Oh! I can testify to the truth of that, for when all my friends have seemed to forsake me then hath the Lord taken me up."

15th. After passing through a low and deeply depressed season, she said, " If I should be taken now, all will be well, I have such a full assurance that there is a mansion prepared for me, and that crowns all." To one of her daughters, " Thou must try and give me up, pray for patience and resignation, and look to the Lord for strength, to say, ' He gave and He can take away, blessed is the name of the Lord.' If thou lookest to Him, thou wilt be preserved, He will never leave thee nor forsake thee." " How tenderly I am dealt with, I am sinking so gradually away." To her grandson, " We have always been tenderly united, and have loved each other, thou wilt feel the loss of me, but be a good boy, be kind to thy parents, and regard those tender impressions thou hast so often felt; encourage them, then thou wilt make a good man."

Being asked the next morning how she felt, she replied, " I want to feel quite resigned;"—shortly after, on recovering from a violent fit of coughing, by which she was much exhausted, " Now I think I can give you all up freely." She gave much suitable advice to a friend who called to see her, and urging the necessity of obedience to manifested duty, that thus he might become qualified to step into the places of those further advanced in age, when they should be laid in the silent grave. Referring to herself, "My only confidence is in my Saviour."

On the 17th, she began to revive, and so far recovered as to be able to pay several visits to her friends.]

12th mo. 31st. The reflecting time is come to part with the past, and enter on the new year : how sweetly consoling, if we have a firm belief, that we have followed the Lamb faithfully in the discharge of all our religious duties, in the year that is over, and cannot be recalled, then our peace will flow as a river, and encourage us to lift up our prayers to our Almighty Helper, that he will be pleased in future to be our shield, and to cover us with the mantle of his love.

1836, 1st mo. 5th. I have been several weeks prevented attending our little meeting from indisposition, yet I have enjoyed a precious stillness in sitting alone; and hope I can say in truth, the Lord has been near, and in tender mercy quieted my mind, and raised the language in my heart, "What shall I render unto thee for all thy benefits, for they are new every morning."

3rd mo. 5th. I have of late experienced many seasons of poverty and want; infirmities of body, and strippedness of mind have been much my companions, and proved my faith and patience, especially at my advanced age, standing as at the brink of the grave. The cry of my heart is, "Let not thy hand spare, nor thine eye pity, until my strong will is slain, and brought into subjection, and all within me is made to bow at thy sacred footstool, and to offer unto thee a living sacrifice, that I might see how good it is to

suffer; had it been otherwise, I might never have enjoyed a feast of fat things.

5th mo. 22nd. I went to London, and attended five
sittings of the Yearly Meeting. I desired that the day
might dawn as formerly, when Truth reigned over
all. The concluding meeting of ministers and elders
was the last that dear Thomas Shillitoe was able to
attend. I had the comfort of his company to Tottenham, and observed he was sinking fast. It may be
truly said, his sun went down in brightness. He
finished a valuable life on the 5th of 6th month.
" Blessed are the dead that die in the Lord, yea, saith
the Spirit, that they may rest from their labours, and
their works do follow them."

6th mo. 14th. I had a pleasant ride home. After
a long dry season, a bountiful Providence was pleased
to water the thirsty ground, and cause a fresh and
lively verdure to renew its beauty. The little birds
were warbling their sweet notes as of joy and praise,
which brought to my mind the words, " The winter is
over and gone, the flowers appear on the earth, the
time of the singing of birds is come, and the voice of
the turtle is heard in our land."

7th mo. 1st. —— and myself went to a Union house
in our neighbourhood, that was to receive the destitute
poor from twenty parishes. The women's side was
nearly uninhabited, but a considerable number of aged
men were there; one of them was reading the Holy
Scriptures, the others sitting by in a becoming manner. We saw their beds and pillows of straw; their
food coarse, but wholesome and clean. Several of
them expressed thankfulness for being provided for in

the decline of life; many of them more than eighty
years of age. I sat a while with them, for my heart
was affected with a sense of our dear Saviour's sufferings, in giving up his precious life for this part of
the creation, who are equally with us, the objects of
his tender care. He came to seek and to save those
that are lost. I believe there are none, either among
the young or the aged, who are not capable of religious impression: but O! that the manifestation of
the light given to every one may not become clouded
by their teachers, many of whom seemed to me to be
better acquainted with forms and ceremonies, than
concerned to lead a self-denying life, and to walk with
the meek and lowly Jesus. I came home reflecting
on my many blessings, and enjoyed my penny.

In the 1st mo. last, an apprehension of duty settled
on my mind, that it would be required of me to pay a
visit to the families of Friends of this Monthly Meeting,
and many times it came with considerable clearness
and weight. My age and infirmities stood much in
my way, not enough considering that the Great
Master, whom I desire to serve, and who, I believed
required the sacrifice, knows my poor weak frame,
and is able to afford strength to perform it.

7th mo. 12th. Monthly Meeting at Dover. As it
approached, I believed the time was come that I
should throw my burden on my friends. But O! for
ever adored be the Great Helper, ever mindful of the
little fearful ones who feel that they have none to cry
to for help, but Him alone, the weight much decreased.
Whilst at my friend's, and in the night, the prospect
closed. In returning home I felt much relieved, and

bowed in humility and thankfulness. Is there any
God like unto our God, who is glorious in holiness,
fearful in praises, working wonders?

31st. I ·went to meeting this morning in much
weakness and fear, lest I should fall a prey to the
devourer. Instead of feeling ability to encourage
others, I longed for the help of their spirits, and said
in my heart, Give me patience, O Lord, to bear the
turnings of thy holy hand upon me. Lead me to
the Rock that is higher than I. This, in unutterable
condescension, was my joyful experience. Oh! what
shall I render unto the God of my salvation for all
his mercies to one so totally unworthy of the least
portion of his tender regard! This renewed abounding
of his love rested with sweetness on my mind many
days—praised be his adorable and great name, both
now and for ever, saith my soul.

8th mo. 28th. Going to meeting this morning in a
degree of passiveness, my vessel was replenished with
a little wine of the kingdom. In the evening, I was
enabled to say from precious experience, "my
Redeemer liveth, blessed be his name who is dealing
thus bountifully. That he may be pleased to carry
on, and perfect his own work, is what my soul craves.

9th mo. 4th. Relieved my mind of a burden that
has long been heavy, on account of a few children
being deprived of the privilege of attending week-day
meetings; their parents not enough considering the
importance of presenting their tender charge before
the Lord on a week-day. We know not when it may
please their heavenly Father most powerfully to visit
and tender their susceptible minds. But how many

coverings there are, that sorrowfully dim the bright shining of that precious light within us, that is lighted by the Divine Light and Life himself, and was never intended to be covered by a bushel, but set on a candlestick, and it giveth light to all that are in the house, not only to our little Society, but those that observe our general conduct through life. If our dear children's teachers were made acquainted with the cause of their absence from school, it might be a means of brightening the light in them, and of inviting them to come, taste, and see for themselves how good the Lord is, and worthy of adoration, worship, and obedience, now and for ever.

7th. When we first sat down in meeting, the precious children being with us, a very sweet feeling covered my mind, wherein I silently mused my heavenly Father's praise : he is a rich rewarder for every act of obedience! I said in my heart, Return to the place of thy rest, O my soul, for the Lord thy God hath dealt bountifully with thee.

[In the 12th month.] This dear invalid was again visited with severe illness, which she was enabled to bear with great patience and resignation, frequently addressing those who attended her with much humility when the following expressions were collected.

12th mo. 19th, 1836. It is an awful thing to appear before the Judge of the whole earth, I am sure I have not a rag to cover myself with, but my whole and entire dependence is on my holy Saviour, who, I humbly hope will plead my cause : I do believe love will cover the judgment seat. If there are any who slight the offers of a merciful Saviour, how deplorable must be their condition!" "I have such sweet sentences of scripture brought to my remembrance, that I think are too good to belong to me." "We have been mercifully dealt with, and blessed in basket and in store; and I firmly believe, that He who has been with me all my life long, will be near and protect my children."

22nd. Addressing her children, "I can leave you to the protection of the Shepherd of Israel, who never will forsake you, unless you first draw back and forsake Him—a father to the fatherless, and a husband to the widow, is God in his holy habitation." "I am of the mind of Job Scott, that man cánnot pray, man cannot of his own natural abilities, pray as he ought."

"I felt so stripped and emptied this afternoon, that I wanted you, my dear children, to come and sit quietly with me, and try to unite our exercise. I have often remembered the positive injunction and promise of our blessed Lord, 'Seek, and ye *shall* find, (no hesitation,) ask, and ye shall receive.' I have felt the Comforter as at the threshold of the door, waiting to do his own office. May we neither of us suffer our eyes to close until we have lifted up our hearts to thee, O thou most adorable Lord God! look down upon us at this most awful time, be near and strengthen us, even the very weakest amongst us, with the influences of thy Spirit; send us help from thy sanctuary, and strengthen us out of Zion!"

24th. "Oh! what a poor creature I am, but my heavenly Father can do all for me. I feel quite willing to go, not at all afraid; and when more

E

depressed and low than I know how to bear, the word is, ' I will never leave thee, nor forsake thee.' "

At another time, " I have a hope, a confirming hope, that a mansion is prepared for me; it is all through the intercession of my dear Redeemer! He sometimes comes in so sweetly. When he does, it is all in mercy, not from merit, I am sure it is always in love unutterable."

25th. " When the Divine power and influence is withdrawn, which is often the case, I feel very low, but when it returns, it is so sweet and reviving!" " How awful is eternity! I am often ready to say, O, eternity, eternity! how inexpressibly awful art thou!" " Oh, how animating is the prospect, to think of joining that innumerable company whom no man can number!"

28th. When feeling very low, she said, " Oh ! to be clothed with the saints' robe of righteousness !"

1st mo. 5th, 1837. After reading the Scriptures, and sitting in silence, " We have had a comfortable little meeting together. We who have leisure, ought to think it our duty to meet more than once a day for this purpose : it seems like an evening sacrifice. Gather up the fragments that nothing be lost."

To one of her children, she said, " I want to tell thee how comfortable I felt in the night, that all was peace ; I had an evidence, (if I dare call it so, to such a poor creature,) that all would be well ; and O, those beautiful gates, if we ever enter, it must be in this humble view of ourselves, it must be so to me, a poor creature, a worm and no man. And you, my dear children, in a particular manner, live in love one with another, and live near that humbling Power that will preserve you. I feel so calm, it seems as if I had nothing to do."

The weakness of her almost exhausted frame, was at times very trying, and she often said, " O, that I may be preserved in patience. O, that it may please my heavenly Father to take me to himself. I hope that speaking of my bodily infirmities will not be considered murmuring; for although I feel more low and languid than I ever have done, my mind is comfortable, I seem to have nothing to do—all appears done for me by a merciful Saviour, by an adorable Redeemer."

From this illness she so far recovered as to be able to attend meetings generally, till the severity of the season prevented, * yet she still enjoyed the company of her friends.

1837, 4th mo. 23rd. Musing on my pillow this morning, I could but commemorate the boundless love of a faithful Creator to my poor soul, from early life to the present day; He made me sensible of his goodness, and inclined me to love and fear Him. I was tendered and broken in meetings, and took opportunities to get alone and strew my tears before the Lord, many times thinking, Oh! that I had lived in the day our blessed Saviour was upon the earth, I would have added one to the number of the multitude that followed him closely, I should have seen his miracles, and loved him more. It often came into my

* On returning, she often remarked the weighty solid deportment of a dear friend, during meetings, who is now removed from time to eternity; also his great care in not entering into light conversation on leaving them.

mind, in days of distress and besetment, "Seek first
the kingdom of heaven, and the righteousness thereof,
and all other things needful shall be added." This
animating promise has often been a consolation to my
drooping spirit In proving seasons when I have
been tried as to an hair's breadth, it was sealed upon
my mind, that if I strove with all my might, if I
kept hold of the anchor, I should be helped through
my deepest conflicts, which has been brought to
pass in a wonderful manner. A compassionate Protector afforded strength to cry unto Him for help,
that he would never leave me, nor forsake me, but
reduce, and humble my soul to this state, Not my
will, but thine be done, O Lord.

5th mo. 3rd. I have been favoured with a comfortable refreshing meeting. Bow very low, O my
soul, and from time to time fully submit under the
refinings of God's power. Oh! with what earnestness
do I desire to have my prayers ascend before him,
that he would continue to be with, and watch
over me now in my feeble old age—protect and
preserve me in a state of subjection to his holy law,
where pride, anxiety, and woe cannot enter—appoint
my dwelling in the low valley, where the grass is
green, and the fragrant flowers give a sweet smell.
Assured I am, that none that ever seek him earnestly in the secret of their minds, but will find him
a God nigh at hand, and graciously disposed to
replenish and satisfy the hungry soul.

7th. I was favoured with the privilege of sitting
with my friends at meeting, and thankful to partake
of a few crumbs, of which I felt very unworthy.

Lord suffer me never to forget thy favours, and clothe my mind with humility; centre me deeper much deeper in it.

9th. We are looking for our Friends to attend a Monthly Meeting here. My earnest desire this morning is to be preserved in a state of watchfulness, that I sin not with my tongue, or prove a stumbling to any, especially to the tenderly beloved young Friends, whose faces are happily turned Zionward. I feel earnest to be preserved from hurting the work of the Lord in myself, or hindering its growth in others. But Oh! thou God of everlasting love, author of every comfort and consolation, reprove and instruct me by the operation of thy pure Spirit in my soul, enable me to say, "I live, yet not I, but Christ liveth in me!"

I was rejoiced to see my valued friend, William Rickman, in the 93rd year of his age; it may be truly said, he is fresh and green in old age; and out of the good treasure of his heart, he was strengthened to bring forth to our comfort: bless the Lord, O my soul, and forget not all His mercies; for He shall be called the repairer of breaches, the restorer of paths to dwell in.

Since the 11th mo. last year, I have had but little opportunity or inclination to make memorandums, and have been often prevented attending meetings through indisposition; but sitting by myself, endeavouring to unite with my Friends who are enjoying the inexpressible privilege of social worship, I have often felt poor and stripped of every sensible feeling of good. "By whom shall Jacob arise, for he is small?" After long striving to wait quietly, the good Remembrancer has

been pleased to prove Himself to be near, and I have
found such seasons to be the means of deep humiliation to my poor forgetful mind. In these baptizing
seasons, the words of a faithful servant of the Lord
have often strengthened me, " Patience in low times
is an excellent anchor, and hope bears up the soul."

10th mo. 1st. I arose this morning very weak and
poorly ; my poor tabernacle is fast declining by age
and infirmities. I can reverently acknowledge that
goodness and mercy have followed me all the days of
my life. Thou, O gracious Helper, hast been with
me through many tribulations, many perils within and
without; I pray thee be with me the remaining part of
my life, and forsake me not, now health and strength
fail : but enable me to live looser from the world, and
closer unto thee, O thou Father and Fountain of every
comfort and consolation. Permit me, O Lord, reverently to covet thy holy protection for myself, my
children, and tender grand-children, that they may be
preserved strangers to the vanities of the world, pride,
and superfluity of every kind. Keep them, I pray
thee, from taking their flight as into the air, where
the snares of the prince of the power thereof are laid to
catch them—keep them from aspiring unto things too
high for them—Oh! most merciful Father, keep us
all, I humbly pray thee, little in our own estimation ;
for thou art God, with the dear Son of thy love blessed
for ever!

10th mo. 11th. —— paid us a very agreeable visit.
How instructive is a growth in grace; the path of the
just shineth brighter and brighter as they diligently
walk in the light; and by every act of obedience they

grow stronger and stronger, but negligence in per-
forming our duty leaves us more in Satan's power.
How needful then is it, to be steadily pressing after
the Father's love, which is the spiritual light and life
of men, and to be watchful unto prayer, to feel the
mind secretly breathing after it. If this is our engagement, and the true hunger and thirst experienced, we
shall be fed.

26th. Sitting up in bed, my mind was very unex-
pectedly comforted by these words, " The Lord knoweth them that are his," which affected me. I said in
my heart, What have I to return for such favours;
surely nothing but shame and confusion of face!

11th mo. 21st. What a favour would it be, if in
our daily retirements we were owned by that enriching
peace, which the world can neither give nor take away.
" Trust in the Lord with all thy heart, and lean not
to thy own understanding"—" Wait on the Lord, be
of good courage and he shall strengthen thine heart,
wait I say on the Lord."—Oh! may it please Him to
raise up judges as at the first, and counsellors as at
the beginning—to hasten that day when truth and
righteousness shall cover the earth as the waters cover
the sea! A participation of the love of God by the
members of the true church, teaches them to know the
communion of saints, and the deep union of the one
Spirit, which makes them as epistles written in one
another's hearts, which neither time nor distance can
ever erase.

In the 3rd month, I heard of the decease of dear
Ann Ransome, of Hitchen. I have not heard of the
particulars of her close, but I have known her to be a

diligent labourer in the Lord's vineyard, and very ser-
viceable in the church discipline. The intelligence
brought to my mind a fresh call to arise and trim my
lamp, that I might not be like the foolish virgins that
were excluded from entering in to behold the Bride-
groom of souls.

Oh! the necessity of not only receiving the seed of
the kingdom, but with all readiness to allow its growth.
The work of truth in the heart of man is described to
be progressive, first the blade, then the ear, then the
full corn in the ear.

There are many publications in this day that have a
tendency to corrupt the mind; if we read the Scriptures they will draw us nearer to God than any other
volume. In the records of our dear Saviour's life and
death, we shall perceive where the Master's feet have
trod; and, in reading his sufferings with attention, the
youthful mind is often moved and tendered, and in
great humility brought nearer to His pure spirit in the
heart.

O Thou that hast been pleased to lengthen out my
days to old age, thou knowest Satan's desire to have
me, that he may sift me as wheat. Oh! suffer me to
know an increase of strength by thy power, which only
is able to support the mind, when the waves of affliction run high, and threaten to overwhelm: it is the
voice of thy omnipotence only that can at such seasons
effectually proclaim, Peace be still!

6th mo. Sitting up in bed, I feel my strength declining. Oh! for patience and firm confidence in my
dear Redeemer, is what I have been striving for, and
hope more fully to attain. But Oh! how poor and

forsaken I am, comparable to the state of Mary of old, in her mournful search. " They have taken away my Lord, and I know not where they have laid him." Oh! grant a continued exercise of soul, until I have found Him whom my soul loveth, because He, first in his adorable goodness and tender mercy, followed me by his heart-reaching calls in the days of my youth, saying, " This is the way, walk in it." I desire more than ever to search closely the most secret parts of my own heart. I have to mourn for suffering the fear of man to stay and hinder me, that I have held back when I should have come boldly forward in the Lord's blessed cause. Oh! my short comings, my many omissions and commissions have caused me many hours of sorrow, and bitter cries to the Creator of the ends of the earth for forgiveness. And I trust in the days of humiliation, I was strengthened again to re-new my covenant similar to Jacob, " If thou wilt be with me in the way I go, give me bread to eat, and raiment to put on. Thou shalt be my God, and I will serve thee;" and in his adorable goodness, peace, yea, solid peace, has been restored, and my soul enabled to magnify and adore His great and glorious name, who is God over all blessed for ever. Amen.

8th mo. 18th. First day, my mind sweetly re-freshed by these words, " Give unto the Lord glory and strength; give unto the Lord the glory due unto His name." Oh! be graciously pleased to preserve me, in my weak state, from becoming a prey to the unwearied enemy of my soul. Oh! grant that the same light that was a light to David's feet, and a lantern to his path, may be permitted to guide my

poor soul into a mansion prepared for it in Thy kingdom. Oh! Thou whose tender love and boundless
compassion, I cannot express as I feel it this morning.
Mayst thou keep me little, low, and in thy fear!

10th mo. 30th. I came down stairs weary, and
resting on the sofa, the sun shone very pleasantly, a
precious sense of my heavenly Father's love refreshed
my heart far more than I deserve, but not more than
I covet. " Return unto thy rest, O my soul, for the
Lord hath dealt bountifully with thee."

I long, and that with tears, to unite with those who
are rightly gathered there (at Meeting) ; the promise
still remains unbroken to those that gather into the
sacred name, the power of Truth, that can alone give
strength to overcome and keep down all wandering
thoughts, and so stay and quiet the mind, as to give
ability to worship the Father in spirit and in truth, and
preserve from presenting their bodies in a lifeless form.

Just put into a nice warm bed, and partaking of
many other comforts. Oh! most merciful God, permit me to meditate in Thy law; in it there is life, and
in it there is joy for evermore!

My mind has been sweetly mingling with my dearly
beloved Father's spirit in heaven—oh! that I could
keep and abide there for ever with my beloved off-
spring!

4th mo. 13th, 1839. My poor head is in much
pain—oh! the most earnest desire of my heart is, that
my merciful Creator and Preserver may be pleased, in
his great love, to keep alive my spiritual senses,
though it may please him to lay low and abase every
other faculty.

20th. Oh! the harmony there is in the Lord's family! " Ephraim shall not envy Judah, nor Judah vex Ephraim"—" they shall not hurt nor destroy in all my holy mountain!"

From this time she was almost wholly confined to her house, and continued gradually to decline till the 9th mo., when she was visited by an only brother, who, after a few days' illness, was removed by death. This unexpected event so forcibly operated upon her, as not only to deprive her of her usual vivacity of mind, but subjected her to much increase of suffering, and the loss of her mental powers, though at times she was favoured with lucid intervals, during which she expressed to the following effect :—

" Oh! that I might die the death of the righteous, and that my latter end might be like theirs."

" Oh! that it may please my heavenly Father to say, ' It is enough !' I have a hope that casteth out fear—I have a hope both sure and stedfast."

" Oh! it is an awful thing to appear before the Judge of the whole earth, but I do not feel afraid, I have a merciful Saviour. My pain is very great, pray for me, that patience may hold out to the end."

A few days before her death, she said, " I must die the death,—our blessed Saviour died the death,—mine is a natural death, but his was for the whole world. He gave up his life freely, and suffered on the cross. He gave his life a willing sacrifice, and we must give up our whole hearts—no cross, no crown, is a sure testimony ; if we will not bear the cross, we cannot have the crown." Then addressing her children, " Oh! my dear children, may you never rest but in the wrestling of the soul, until He has fully redeemed you, until He has finished the work He has begun in you. Oh! from my dying bed, I beg of you, that it may be the earnest breathing of your souls, that you may be redeemed from the perishing things of time, and that your affections may be fixed upon eternity: upon things that will endure for ever. What would it avail me now (or any at such a time as this) to have the world, or as much as might be equal to our most extravagant desires to possess? we would freely give it up in exchange for a happy possession! Oh! press after it; do not be satisfied in any thing that is sensual or carnal, but oh! that we may press after an inheritance in that which will endure for ever!"

" Oh, Eternity! oh! the length of eternity! oh! that it may be impressed on every heart the length of eternity! *There is no end!*"

She peacefully expired the 25th of 1st mo., at her house at Ashford in Kent, and was interred in Friends' burial ground there, the 2nd of 2nd mo., 1840.

" The salvation of the righteous is of the Lord: he is their strength in the time of trouble. And the Lord shall help them, and deliver them : He shall deliver them from the wicked, and save them, because they trust in him."—Psalm xxxvii. 39, 40.

JOHNSTON & BARRETT, Printers, 13, Mark Lane.

CPSIA information can be obtained
at www.ICGtesting.com
Printed in the USA
BVHW041407011220
594599BV00015B/1795